AF472333

Fifteen - Two
A Memoir

By James E Parenteau
with James P Parenteau

www.aviationcommentary.com, Beaumont, California

Cover Design © 2010 by Paul W. Newell

ISBN: 978-0-557-85978-8

Printed in the United States of America

10 9 8 7 6 5 4 3 2 1

JAMES E. PARENTEAU
BORN 4 NOVEMBER 1921
SUPERIOR, WISCONSIN
PART 1

CHAPTER 1

THE EARLY YEARS

My first recollection was as a child under the age of five living in Spooner, Wisconsin. I was playing with another boy my age. We were running around the house in opposite directions. We met at the corner of the house and ran smack into each other. I received a bloody nose and ran crying to my mother for help.

We later moved to Superior, Wisconsin. We moved into a house where upon moving in we found a bird in the house. My mother was very frightened and told us that a bird in the house was the sign that a death would occur in that house. That frightened me at the time and I never forgot that experience.

My next recollection was at age five. I attended the Allouez grade school in kindergarten. I believe the school was the Franklin School. We lived in a small house just about a half block from the school. My teachers name was Miss McCombs. She was a pretty lady and a kind teacher. That winter my two older brothers, Art and Roy, built a snow house in the shape of an igloo. They made a ski run from the top of that igloo down the backside. They then made ski marks and wet them down so they would be icy. I was advised that I was to stay off their ski run with my sled. Later when no one was round, I climbed up to the top of the igloo with my sled. Knowing that I would be in trouble if I damaged their ski run, I decided to slide down the front side of the igloo (the side that has the entrance to the igloo on it). I thought when my sled met the ground it would keep on going and I would have a nice ride. My sled had a wooden apple box attached to it. I kneeled down on the sled behind the apple box and pushed off. When we hit the ground, the sled stopped and I hit my nose on the wooden box. My nose was broken and bleeding. I screamed and ran for the house. My mother nearly fainted when she saw me. She called my Uncle Jack who came over and held me while the doctor stitched my nose back together. That was a memorable experience for a five year old.

We moved from that house on Second Street to a larger house with wooden sidewalks on First Street in Allouez. Since I was Catholic, I stated the first grade in the St. Anthony School in Allouez. At about age seven, I was sitting on a woodpile watching Art and Roy playing baseball with a couple of their friends. One of them was knocking flies to the others. He tossed the ball up into the air and swung the bat at the ball and missed it. The bat slipped out of his hands and flew about fifteen feet through the air and struck me across the face. The cut I received on my right eyebrow required stitches. A few days later, I still had the eye bandaged when I made my First Communion in the Catholic Church. The picture they took of me all dressed up in a suit with the bandage on the right eye on that occasion is still in my possession.

We moved to another house on Itasca Street in Allouez during my grade school years. While living on Itasca Street, we lived closer to the school. One memory while at that house was on one occasion when I wanted to go fishing down at Lake Superior Bay. My mother refused to let me go. I then climbed out of the bathroom window and went fishing anyhow. While fishing, I slipped off the boat dock and fell into the water and although someone grabbed me and pulled me out, I have a feeling that I came near to drowning since I could not swim at all at that time. I do not know how deep the water was but believe it was six to eight feet deep. I recall that I believed that I had been punished for sneaking away from home when I was told that I could not go.

On certain days of the week, if a person took a container to the Catholic school they would fill your container with free buttermilk. I remember how happy I was to be able to take the metal half-gallon container to the school and have it filled with buttermilk and take it home to my father. He loved buttermilk. Frankly, I hated the taste of buttermilk and still do to this day. I didn't understand how he could drink it.

1931
Jim First Communion Sunday.
God must have been pleased when he looked down and saw this.
Notice bandage on left eye. Also wood sidewalks.

We were to leave Wisconsin with our parents and travel by automobile to White Bear Lake, Minnesota for a weeks stay. We had a carload of children by this time. While we were visiting in White Bear Lake we received a telephone call from our Uncle Jack saying that our house had caught on fire. In listening to the conversations, I was to believe that between my father, his brother in law Archie Lemier (in building construction in Minnesota) and my Uncle Jack, the house was set on fire for the insurance they held on that house. My Uncle Jack happened to be in the neighborhood and was the one that noticed the house burning at two or three o'clock in the morning and notified the fire department. The cause of the fire was storage of old oily rags in the closet under the stairway. I have no proof that this was the case but I have a very strong belief that this was true. When we returned home, we children were separated from our parents for a few weeks. We were sent to various relatives to live temporarily while they located another house to rent. I was the only one to go to the home of the Lavadier's to stay with Aunt Flora and her family. It was an unhappy experience.

We moved to a small house located just a couple of blocks behind the St. Anthony School where we lived for a couple of years. I was probably in the fifth and sixth grade there. During that time, I was to become an altar boy who assisted in what we called serving Mass. I was to learn to recite prayers in Latin. I learned them phonetically but never knew what they meant I could recite them real fast: for example Ah Diem Que Le Tiffy Cot Uven Tutum Mayum, Qua Re May Re Poliste (etc.). It made me feel important to get up at 5:00 AM to serve at the 5:30 AM Mass. I later found out that if you volunteered, you would be chosen to assist the Priest in conducting funeral services at the cemetery. I knew that if you did assist at the funeral services the family would give you money. I always volunteered and was very happy to earn money in this manner.

Another experience I had at the school was that I was chosen to sing a duet for the eighth grade graduating class banquet. Another boy and I sang the duet together. It was my first performance as a singer and I was scared to perform and was very happy when it was over.

There was another time when I was attending a bazaar at the school. Someone gave me a few nickels for spending money. I put a nickel on a number and they spun the wheel and I won a large ham that I proudly took home to my mother for a family meal of ham.

I was able to get an opportunity to sell the Sunday Newspaper "The Milwaukee Journal" every Sunday. I would carry the newspapers down to the Iron Ore Docks and would climb a high ladder that ran from the dock up to the deck of the Iron Ore Boat. It was a ladder that was high above the water at points. If I had fallen, I would have fallen into about 90 feet of water that was the depth that an iron ore boat needed at dockside when loaded with ore. I would sell several papers on the boat. One time, a sailor gave me a dollar tip. That was really something in those days. I really enjoyed selling newspapers.

In 1932 at age eleven, I was beginning to believe that due to our large family we were considered to be under privileged children and in fact lived in a poor family. My mother had eight children at that time. I was the fourth oldest of the children.

During the summer of 1932, my father was out of work and we were to leave Allouez and move out to Dreamland about fifteen miles out of town. Bill O'Brien, owner of the O'Brien Oil Company in Itasca, owned a house on the highway. There were two gasoline pumps and a small station on the front part of the property adjacent to the highway. Arrangements were made for our family to live there and run the gas station for Mr. O'Brien. I remember that my father had a large amount of change that he placed on his bedroom dresser every night when he went to bed. I learned that if one took a small amount of money from his dresser it went unnoticed. Later my sister, Evelyn, and I would be dropped off with a family in Allouez to play with their children while my parents went grocery shopping in Superior. I used that money to buy candy and cigarettes for all of us. Evelyn was a smoker then but I hadn't yet gotten the habit. I was never caught for this act because I never took but small amounts of his change. One time on our return trip from grocery shopping, I rode on the four-wheel trailer that my Dad pulled with his car. The trailer had lots of food on it including a couple of 50-pound sacks of flour. We were traveling down a two-lane highway on a state route. I was lying down in the trailer when I felt something hit my hand. I looked up to see the trailer had become loose from the car. I watched as it veered left across the oncoming lane of the highway and off the highway. At this point, the metal tongue of the trailer went into the ground and the trailer came to an abrupt stop. Everything including me was thrown forward clear off the trailer. I landed on one of the sacks of flour, which had broken open and I was covered with flour. I was not injured and got up to see the car continuing on its trip home. Apparently no one inside the car noticed that I was no longer with him or her. The car was gone for what seemed like a long time. I wondered how far they would go before someone noticed that the trailer and I were no longer with them. They finally came back and got me and the groceries and the trailer. Possibly the nut holding the trailer hitch to the car was actually what I had felt hit my hand when the trailer came loose from the car. Fortunately, there was not much traffic on that highway. If another had hit the trailer automobile while crossing that traffic lane I would probably not have survived. That was a thrill and experience that I was never to forget.

In 1933 we moved back to town into another house that was located on Sixth Street in East End, Superior, Wisconsin. The house was a very large structure with many bedrooms. It was next door to a Protestant Church. The minister and his family lived just behind the church. I was aware that my father who was a Fireman on the Chicago Northwestern Railroad worked only an occasional day every now and then. Because of the longevity system on the railroad he only worked about three or four days a month. We did not have any money but apparently were able to charge groceries at the Seventh Street Market and seemed to have enough to eat. The house was very large and very difficult to heat. We had a space heater in the living room downstairs and sitting around the stove was sometimes the only warm place in the house. I observed that my father had ways to cut down on the expenses of operating a household. For example, I learned that if you run a wire from the incoming electric lines, around the electric meter and plug it into a light socket in the kitchen, you are able to by-pass the meter and can use all the electricity you want and it does not register on the meter. This procedure also obviously by-passed the protection provided by the fuse box and fuses. We were fortunate in that no problems resulted from this procedure.

I also saw my father physically disconnect the gas meter, which was located inside the kitchen in the house. He would disconnect the entire meter and with gas shooting out of the incoming pipe right into the kitchen, he would turn the meter around and reconnect the pipes again. This would reverse the in and out connections of the meter. I do not know if this reversed the meters and made them run backward or not but running the meters in this manner allowed him to use gas without having to pay for it. This action actually resulted in a very low gas bill. This procedure was to work very well and would have continued had we not had a fire break out in the kitchen when the gas ignited during one of the times when he was turning the meter around. There was no damage to the house as a result of the fire, but my dad did have minor burns to his arms. He had to call for help in turning the gas off at the curb. Shortly thereafter, our gas meter was relocated outside the house where their employees who were sometimes in the area could watch it more closely.

I attended the seventh and eighth grade at the St. Francis Xavier Catholic School in East End. We lived across the street from the Euclid Hotel parking area, which was dirt and cinders. Our major activities were playing marbles on a daily basis during the marble season. We also played tin can baseball, hide and seek and various other games. I remember friends' names like Horace Greely, Red Hayes, and girls like Mary Jane Ward and Jean Stephenson during those years. I graduated from the eighth grade in 1935.

During the Christmas holidays, in the year 1935, on a normal winter evening, we children were playing in the house. My two-year-old brother Harold was spinning around until he would stagger and we would all laugh. Later that night, we were awakened to a flurry of activity and found out that my brother Harold was very ill. My father frantically called the doctor which was a waste of time, since we had no money, the doctor would not make it in time to help my brother. I had held Harold lying across my lap while my dad was massaging him to try and get him to breathe properly. Harold died that night before the doctor arrived at our house. We went back to bed and I remember how sad and angry I was when they carried Harold out of the house later that Christmas Eve. Harold died on 24 December 1935. That was to put a damper on our Christmas celebrations for a couple of years. To this day, I cannot stand to see a child spin around until they get dizzy, although I know that had not been the cause of Harold's death.

We again moved to another house during the summer of 1936. This time we moved to a house just off Stinson Avenue on Tenth Street in East End. We lived in this house until after I graduated from High School in 1939. As you can imagine, I have many more memories of this period of my life than I had during the previous years.

It was not long after we moved into the house on Tenth Street that I was to meet Henry (Hank) Zielinski. Hank lived on Tenth Street about a half block off Stinson Avenue in the opposite direction. During my entire years in high school Hank and I were like Siamese Twins. Whenever we left our houses, either one of us, we left together.

Hank was interested in boxing. He was a tough Polish lad who would fight at the drop of a hat. Neither one of us was very big nor very heavy but we learned to fight. We trained with a fight manager in downtown Superior. He had a gym where we worked out along with some professional fighters whom he managed. Once in a while we were used as sparring partners with one of the pros. We also had more than our share of street fights. During my senior year Hank and I both made our weights on the Superior East High School boxing team. We had several amateur ring fights against other high school competitors. Hank won all of his fights by knockouts. I won all but one of my fights by decision. The fight I lost was also by a decision. I never really had Hank's killer instinct. When Hank got into a fight he was out to kill from the start. I usually got off to a slow start until I got hurt. Then I threw all caution to the wind and went after my opponent like I really meant business. We each earned a high school letter in boxing. I still have my boxing letter today. I learned early in life that when you are in a fight, either boxing or street fighting, the pain is not very bad. When you get hurt fighting, the body system goes into shock and you do not feel any real pain until later on when the fight is over.

CHAPTER 2

HIGH SCHOOL

I was age fourteen to seventeen during my high school years between 1936 and my graduation from school in 1939. The following experiences happened to me during those years. I don't believe it is important which one of the events happened in what order so I will not try and date them.

Neither Hank nor I had any money at the time during those years. If we wanted to see a movie we had to sneak into the theater while the people were exiting between features. We were sometimes successful but most of the time the usher would catch us and put us out of the theater. When we went to a high school football game we had to climb over the fence and drop in behind the grandstand. There were people patrolling the fence on the inside but we waited until they walked by and we would make a hurried attempt to get in over the fence. Most of the time they would not be able to apprehend us as we quickly mixed in with the crowd.

Since we did not have any money, our recreation after dinner each evening was hanging around the streets with about three or four of our friends. We could almost always count on meeting our friends on Second Street (the main street) in East End. Hank and I would join the group if we found them or we would find something to do by ourselves if we did not meet up with them. We often did some things that could get us into trouble. We were usually never apprehended doing them. We did have a bad reputation with the local East End police. It wasn't unusual to have them pick us up and take us to the East End police station for questioning but we were usually let go our own way after just a short questioning period.

Many evenings we would hitchhike a ride to downtown Superior and bum around downtown. We were usually able to get a ride downtown, several miles away. If we didn't get a lift we wouldn't bother to go. However, after we got downtown it was more like ten or eleven PM when we started home. We usually had to walk home. On one occasion, we were walking and hitchhiking from downtown Superior to East End and were held up by a slow moving freight train crossing Belnap Avenue. We decided on the spur of the moment to jump into a boxcar because we knew the train went right by our house. We planned to jump out of the boxcar when we reached our house. To our surprise, the train was going about forty miles an hour when we went through East End. We were very worried because we couldn't jump at that speed and for all we knew the train might be going to Chicago. We had no choice but to stay aboard. The train had to slow down when it crossed a river south of East End. When it slowed down we decided that as soon as we crossed the river we would jump before it could resume speed. We jumped and neither of us was hurt. My father was waiting up for me when I got home and I was to be very sorry that I had taken that long way home.

On another occasion, on New Years Eve Hank and I were walking down Tower Avenue (main street in Superior) and a man asked us if we had a light. Without discussing it, Hank said, “let's take him.” Hank hit him and I knew I had to help him so I joined in also. The man did not try to fight the two of us and quickly turned and ran away. We had no idea who he was. About three months later, on an afternoon on a rare occasion when Hank and I were not together, that man caught me alone on Main Street in East End. He said “I'll be you aren't as tough when you and your friend aren't together. Step out into the alley with me.” He was much bigger than I was and weighed twice as much as I but I went with him to take my medicine. Much to my surprise, I was able to beat him to the punch for a long time. I cut his face up a lot but he was very strong and I could not put him away. Finally, he landed an uppercut catching me square on the mouth and he knocked my two front teeth straight back into my mouth. I didn't get off the ground and he let me off and walked away. I found Hank and we walked up to my brother Art and Roberta's apartment in downtown Superior to get cleaned up. I reached into my mouth and was able to pull the two teeth straight but they were overlapped so I had to push them back in and arrange them so they would not overlap the next time. Roberta says she will never forget that night when she opened the door and saw me with my shirt covered with blood. She washed and dried my clothes so I could go home. I was to lose those two teeth the first time I went to the dentist after I was in the service in 1942.

We never had a nickel of our own so we would take every opportunity we could to steal whatever we wanted to take. Mostly small stuff though. We would steal candy bars in the dime stores and once in a while we would grab a box of candy and run out of the store. In a little store in East End we would go into the store having pooled our pennies and buy a nickel Popsicle. We knew the old man had to turn his back on us to get the popsicle out of the freezer. When he did we loaded a newspaper bag with small pies, candy or whatever we could get our hands on while he was getting the popsicle. We did that many times during a three or four month period. One time my Uncle Jack took me aside and told me that we were to stop stealing from that store of he would see that we were stopped. I do not know to this day how he found out that we were doing the stealing but that was the last we stole anything from that store.

One night we were sitting along side a building in East End and someone suggested that we see if we could break into a small store that night. Hank was with me at the time and he said he was not going to have any part of that deal. Hank went home. The rest of us waited until it was late at night and then went up to a side door to try and get into the store. Red Hayes, one of the guys from our group, had about fifteen keys and some supposedly were pass keys. Red was able to open the door and we went in. The family actually lived behind the store but we knew they had not been home for a couple of days. We went into their quarters and had a good time joking while a couple of the fellows smoked cigarettes. After a while we decided to take a few things with us, as we were getting ready to leave. As we were taking what we wanted out of the glass display cases in the front of the store, we heard someone try the front door. We looked up and it was a policeman making a routine check as he was walking the beat. While he was looking in through the glass door we dropped to the floor. We whispered and decided that he may have heard us. We said "let's make a run for it out the side door." we all got up and ran out the side door and ran toward the back way. We heard the policeman shout, "Stop or I'll shoot!" We did not heed his advice. He did not shoot. To our surprise, we found a fence in the back yard. We climbed over the fence and kept running. We ran about a block to the nearby Catholic School where we could hide and watch them. I had lost my cap when I went over the fence. In a small town like East End I would have been a dead duck if they found my hat. We figured they would be able to trace it to me. We watched as three police cruisers joined the policeman at the store. They were spread out around the building searching the grounds with flashlights. Red Hayes volunteered to creep through the tall grass among the policemen to retrieve my cap if he could find it. We watched and waited until finally Red returned with my cap in his hand. Red said that he had been close enough to the policemen to reach out and grab one by the leg. I was sure glad to see my cap again. We hid the things we had taken from the store and later retrieved them. We never heard anything more about the incident. Hank was glad he had not taken part in that episode.

One of our friends, Torvald Sather's father owned a 1937 Chevrolet. Torv would occasionally get the use of his dad's car. When he did we would cruise around the town. Of course we needed gasoline and once in a while a quart of oil. We became proficient in siphoning gasoline. We would get it from a car parked on the street or from a car parked inside a garage if the people left the garage unlocked. We were never apprehended, although we once got quite a scare when we were in a person's garage and the man came out of the house. We just made a run for it. We did lose our gas can and our hose at that house. Oil was harder to get. In those days it was normal practice for the gasoline stations to stack about twenty quart size cans of oil out by the gasoline pumps and take them in at night when they closed the station. Our only means to get oil was to walk up to a service station, grab a couple cans of oil and run for it. We never were caught doing that either.

We enjoyed cruising the streets better than walking which led us to stealing cars for entertainment and for transportation to get us home at the end of an evening in downtown Superior. Our method of stealing cars was limited to walking along any street of homes wherever we were at the time and looking in each car window to see if the person had left his keys in the car. Then we would try the door. If it were unlocked, Torv would get in and try to start the motor. If it started we would all get in and take off. We would always park the car about a half-mile from home after we finished using it. We were very careful not to do any damage to the cars. One night as we were cruising along, a police car traveling in the opposite direction did a quick U-turn and chased us. We naturally assumed he recognized the stolen car and we made a run for it. We traveled at high speeds even though the icy roads were very slippery but succeeded in out running the police cruiser. After we did, we parked that car and took off. About a year later, we found out that Torvald Sather had stolen a car and headed for Florida. The Kentucky State Police took him into custody when they found him asleep in the car. He had been driving into stations and filling his tank and then taking off without paying for the gasoline. Torv's dad got him off without a jail term but we were never to steal a car gain.

Torv Sather was always trying to convince us that a good way to get spending money was to go "Purse Snatching." I don't remember whether or not Torv had actually grabbed a purse. He did want us to go purse snatching with him. I finally decided that I would go along and give it a try. Hank said he would have no part in that activity. I should have listened to Hank when he would not go for something like this. Torv and I went walking the street s of downtown Superior looking for an opportunity to snatch a purse. Obviously you needed o find a woman who carried her purse loosely and who was all alone on a lonely street that was not too well lighted. The more we walked the more I wished that I had not joined in this venture. We never found a likely candidate that evening and I never was willing to try that again.

One time I drove my dad's car when he hadn't let me use it. I noticed that the gas was low which could lead to questions so I got a can and a hose and siphoned gasoline from a city grader parked near our house. Well at least I thought it was gasoline. The next day my father tried to start the car and it would not start. He made arrangements for a mechanic to repair his car. I went to the mechanic and told him what I had done and he said, "No wonder it won't start, that grader uses diesel fuel. He said I won't tell your dad, I will just take care of it and charge your dad for fixing his car."

Another experience found Paul Tripanier and I downtown in Superior on Tower Avenue just bumming along. Paulie said, "I have to go in and buy me a pair of tennis shoes." I went in the store with him surprised that he had enough money to buy the shoes. His parents had given him the money. We went in and Paulie bought a pair of tennis shoes. As we were leaving the store Paulie grabbed a box of twelve pair of fur lined men's gloves and said, "Run for it." We took off as fast as we could run and were not apprehended. We sold the gloves to people we knew in East End and one pair to a man coming out of a bar. About two weeks later, Paulie and I were sitting in the East End Theater watching a movie and the usher and a policeman came in and took us to the Downtown Superior Jail. We were relieved of all our belongings and each locked up in separate jail cells. After we were in there for a couple hours, they came and got me and took me to the police chief's office for questioning about the robbery of the gloves. He said someone in the store had recognized us and reported us. I confessed to the crime. He then let us go on the condition that we would pick up as many of the pairs of gloves as we could and return them to the police station. We got a friend to pose as a policeman and come with us to each of the people to whom we had sold the gloves and retrieve them. We were able to get all of the gloves except the ones we had sold to the man coming out of the bar. We had no idea who he was. We returned the gloves to the police station and never heard from them again. To our great surprise, the police did not even tell our parents about the incident.

Hank's girlfriend was Marie DeClerk. Marie lived about a mile out Stinson Avenue from our houses. Her father owned the Stinson Avenue Dairy. Marie was the only girlfriend that Hank ever had to my knowledge. It was well known that if anyone tried to move in on Hank's girl, he would have a fight on his hands. A couple of times when someone decided to walk Marie home from school they were faced with a thrashing. Word spread quickly about Marie. My own fate with girlfriends was not as simple. Every time I found a girl whom I really liked, I was soon warned to stay away from her by her older brother. I finally met the only girl I really liked very much. Her name was Betty Lou Swanson. Her father was a captain of an iron ore boat on the Great Lakes. She was an only child. They lived in a mansion. The house had at least 24 rooms.

Betty Lou's mother was an alcoholic and her father was never home. He was gone all summer on the ore boats. I finally started staying with Betty Lou until one or two o'clock in the morning. On all but one occasion I was able to get out of the house before her mother came home. On that night I met her in their yard as I was leaving in the wee hours. She read me the riot act while I just kept walking away. Betty Lou and I went steady for quite a long time. We kept dating even though her mother did not approve of me. One evening when I went to pick up Betty Lou, she wasn't home. I sat on her front porch and waited for her to come home. When she did, Red Hayes' younger brother was escorting her. She went right into the house. I wanted to fight him but he refused to fight. That was the last time I was to date Betty Lou. She wouldn't have anything to do with me anymore. I saw her a couple of years after that when I was home on leave from the service. She was not interested in seeing me again. She later moved to Duluth, Minnesota. I have never seen nor heard from her again.

While living on Tenth Street, my oldest brother would take me along to the softball playing fields on Saturday afternoons. I would play the catcher position. Art always played second base. We had many good afternoons of softball during the summer time. I later in life played catcher on USAF softball teams when I was in the Air Force.

When we moved to Tenth Street, the house had a garage and a small barn in the back yard. My father bought a cow and a lot of chickens. I inherited the job of taking care of the cow. We had a lot of fun with the cow. We did not have a pasture for her. We would take her out in any field where we could get by with it and stake her out. We had a long iron stake that I would put into the ground. The stake had about fifty feet of chain that I would connect to the halter on the cow. Of course the cow would not have any water and when I would go get the cow to take her home to give her a drink, she would take off like a streak for the water. There were times when she would drag me across the ground on my stomach, depending on how thirsty she was. I was to be kidded about that cow on many occasions. She was a good cow though and would give between six and fourteen quarts of milk a day. Along with the eggs and meat from the chickens, and with the eight or nine loaves of bread that my mom baked every other day, we always had food to eat. We also had a large garden that provided vegetables for our meals. The main thing which we did not get very much of was meat. When we had a ring of baloney for dinner, we each got one small piece of meat about an inch wide.

My father was only to work about three days a month. When he worked, he was a fireman on the Chicago and North Western Railroad. When he did work, at least once an evening he would go right by the back of our house. I was always advised that he would be throwing a load of coal off the engine when he would go by the area where we lived. I knew that, before I went to bed that night, I would have to go find the coal and put it in the coal cellar. Some times when we had about two or three feet of snow on the ground, I could see where the large lump of coal went into the snow and I would have to trace it until I found the coal where it stopped rolling. That was a very cold job, not very well liked.

Hank and I started drinking in about the tenth grade. We drank whenever we could get our hands on a forty-cent half pint of liquor or a cheap bottle of wine. We must have had a reputation because on the evening I graduated form high school and was to get my diploma, the high school principal met me and searched me to insure that I didn't have a bottle hidden on my person. I didn't have one so he let me enter the school what he didn't know was that I already had a half pint of whiskey in my school locker for that occasion.

Hank and I were always trying to figure a way to get our hands on some spending money. One evening while we were walking around downtown Superior, we decided that it could be possible to hang around out behind a bar and wait for a good opportunity to come along. For example: if a drunk came out of the bar by himself, we could knock him down and remove his wallet and run for cover. We found a bar and stood out back and watched and waited for our chance that night. Soon a drunk came staggering out of the back door of the tavern, just as we had planned. Hank and I moved in on him. We both hit him at the same time. Hank went for the jaw and I went for the stomach. Well, this fellow didn't just fall quietly down and lay still so we could take his wallet. Instead, he staggered backward about ten feet and fell into a pile of wood. He made so much noise doing so that Hank and I decided to make a run for it. We decided that this was no way to make spending money and never tried that again.

On one occasion during our high school years, a friend of some of the guys we knew (not a personal friend of mine or Hank's) attempted to grab a case of whiskey from a liquor truck that was parked in an alley in Superior during the daylight hours. A policeman saw him and shouted "Stop or I'll shoot!" When he didn't stop the policeman shot him in the back as he tried to run away. I remember the policeman's name was Liebowitz, but I do not remember the name of the boy who was shot. The boy recovered from the gunshot wound and the policeman was highly criticized by the local newspaper for shooting him. We knew that boy but Hank and I had never been involved with him in any way. I remember thinking at the time that this was a good example why we had better stop some of the schemes we would dream up to get spending money.

In 1939 there was a lot of talk about Adolph Hitler in Germany and the trouble he was starting. Hank and I decided to enlist in the Navy. My father refused to sign the necessary papers so I did not go into the Navy. Hank's dad signed the papers and Hank went into the U.S. Navy. He received basic training at the Great Lakes Naval Training Center near Chicago. Hank came home for a short leave after boot camp was finished. When Hank left again for his next assignment with the Navy, I was never to see or talk to him again. I heard news about him, though. He married and divorced a girl in San Francisco. He later married another girl in San Francisco. He lived his life there and like me, for the rest of his life, returned to Superior, Wisconsin only for short visits. I heard that he never had any children. Hank died in his early fifties. I was to find out that he had become an alcoholic and died of cirrhosis of the liver.

The summer after I graduated from high school and after Hank went into the Navy, I went to work at the Seventh Street Market grocery store. I never received any money for working at that store. All of the money I earned was used to help pay my father's grocery bill.

When fall came along, I attended vocational school in Superior where I took classes in typing and in Morse Code. I was able to learn to copy American Morse Code. As a result of these two classes, I was able to get into a Chicago Northwestern Railroad training program with five other young men. We were allowed to move into the ladies waiting room of various railroad depots and actually got practice working as telegraph operators after the railroad stations closed down for the day. I was able to take up residence at the Hawthorne railroad depot along with another of the men in our group for several weeks. At the end of the training period, the railroad had three telegrapher positions to fill. I was not hired. Two of the three men hired were sons of men who were already telegraphers on that railroad.

During the summer of 1940, I went to work at the Stinson Avenue Dairy where Hank's girlfriend lived. I worked from five in the morning until six in the evening seven days a week. My wages were one dollar a day plus room and board. I lived over the garage in a very comfortable sleeping room. I ate all of my meals with the family. I can honestly say that was the first time in my life that I really had all I could eat. We worked hard for our wages. I gave twenty-five dollars a month to Mom to help support the family. The other five dollars was good for a night out once a month.

On one of those nights, when I was out drinking with friends, I was pretty loaded. I was riding along lying down on the back seat of my friend's car. He said "Jim, fix that back window so it doesn't rattle any more." I said "I will fix that window for you" and I kicked my foot through the car window. However, in doing so, I put a deep cut into the back of my ankle. He took me to my house on Tenth Street and we bandaged it up. Then he drove me back to the farm. I was not able to work for a while and when I finally went to the doctor, he said, "Son, you are very lucky that you did not sever the tendon." I had nicked the tendon and it was healing up slowly.

In the fall of 1940 my family moved again. This time they moved to a house in Itasca. It was near the railroad tracks as well. It was a very nice house. About the only experience I can recall in that house was the fact that now we were near the railroad coal shed where they loaded the coal onto the engines. My father told me that

I had to go to the coal shed and steal coal to heat our house. I didn't like that job because it was hard work and often very cold. I decided that I would try very hard to get caught stealing coal so that I would not have to do it any more. I took a toboggan and I left a trail from the coal shed to my house every time I went to steal coal, but I was never apprehended. I really was to believe that the railroad detectives knew that I was taking coal, but they also knew my father and knew he was only taking what he needed to keep his family warm. So they didn't bother me even though I wanted them to stop all the hard work I had to do.

CHAPTER 3

IN THE ARMY NOW

During the fall of 1940, I visited the Army Recruiting Officer in Superior and tried to get into the Army Signal Corps. I was a high school graduate and had training with the railroad copying American Morse Code. The recruiter advised me that I had to obtain three letters of reference. I provided the references and was advised that I would be put on a list of applicants for military service. I was finally accepted by the Service and was given a report date of 9 April 1941.

I had known Bud Leonard in high school. We had been running around together since Hank had joined the Navy. Bud had also applied for Military Duty and had also been given a report date of 9 April. On the 9th of April 1941, Bud Leonard and I, under Military Orders, boarded the passenger train in Superior, Wisconsin. When we arrived in Wausau, we were met and taken to a building where we were given a physical examination and sworn into the U.S. Army. We departed Wausau that same day for Chicago, Illinois. An Army officer picked us up at the depot in Chicago and transported us to an Army Base near Chicago. The next day we traveled by train to the Jefferson Barracks, Missouri Army Base for our basic training. The base was near St. Louis, Missouri. We were taken to a very large building on the base where the sleeping quarters were double-decked beds. I felt like the one room must have slept a thousand men. That night as I went to bed I wanted to leave and go home. I would have done so if I hadn't been sworn in already. I was very homesick and cried a long time before I went to sleep. Within a couple of days Bud and I started our Basic Training. We were moved into tents that slept four men. Every morning at five AM they would wake us up and we would fall out on the Company Street for the start of another day. We would not be able to go out of the area for any reason. After a couple of weeks Bud and I decided we were gong to go to the Base Exchange. We were reported and punished. As punishment we were to work Kitchen Police (K.P.) duties in the Mess Hall for seven days. Our duties in the mess hall started at 5 Am and lasted until ten at night. The work was hard but we got all the food we wanted to eat. We discussed the alternatives and decided that K.P. duty was better than basic training. We managed to occasionally get K.P. work after that and were to miss out on the forced marches and even missed the weapons firing training. We finished our basic training with our group and were transferred to the Army Air Corp Communications School at Scott Field, Illinois in the spring of 1940.

Bud and I were assigned to the 13th Communications School Squadron at Scott Field to attend the Radio Operator and Mechanics Course. We lived in the same barracks. We attended classes to learn to copy International Morse Code. International Morse Code was a totally different code system than the American Morse Code that was used on the railroad. We also studied electricity and radio transmitters and receivers. We learned Air to Ground Communication procedures and many other things.

During that summer, Bud and I talked about taking off after school on Friday and hitchhiking to Superior, Wisconsin for a short visit. This meant going Absent Without Leave (AWOL). We would be gone Saturday, Sunday and return on Monday. We asked a couple of fellows if they would answer roll call for us in the formations that would take place on Saturday and Monday until we returned. They said they would do it if they could. We studied the ramifications and decided it was worth a try. We hitchhiked to Superior and back and the men covered for us. We were not apprehended. It was not long until we decided to try it again. This time, while hitchhiking back we were given a ride by some men who were known as "The Hell Drivers." They treated us to a few drinks too many and Bud and I spent the night in a used car lot sleeping in one of the cars in Racine, Wisconsin. We did not make it back to camp until Tuesday. By that time the men were no longer able to cover for us. We went before the Commanding Officer to receive punishment under the 104th Article of War for being AWOL. Bud was given a week's K.P. and fined $9.00 a month for four months. I was given a week of K.P. Duty but was not fined. I never found out what happened that he was given a fine and I was not. We saw the Commander separately.

We were allowed to go into St. Louis on Saturday night and Sunday. I think it was about fifteen or twenty miles from Scott

Field. On one trip, I had too much to drink and passed out in an alley where I slept it off. When I sobered up somewhat, I awoke to find that my hat and my wallet were both gone. The only thing that saved me was that I had enough change in my pocket to take a bus back to Scott Field. However, when we got to the entrance to Scott Field, the Military Police got on the bust to check our I.D. cards. I was in trouble. I was out of uniform and had no I.D. card. It was in my wallet. I was taken off the bus and taken to the Army Guard House to sleep it off for the night. When I got back to the barracks the next day I found out that Bud and my other buddies had taken my wallet so that no one would rob me. They had gone on with their plans for the evening and when they had come back to take me home, I was gone. I wasn't very happy with myself, or them, but I was happy to get my wallet back.

Bud was washed out of school a few months later and assigned to the Base Supply at Scott Field. I continued my schooling. Bud was moved across the base to another area and I did not see much of him any more.

On another trip to St. Louis I met a good-looking girl. I met her at a bar. I dated her for a while. One night when I went to her house to pick her up her mother answered the door. She asked me if I knew how old her daughter was. I said, "No, I don't know her age." Her mother told me she was fifteen years old. I left immediately never to return to see that girl again. I thought she looked about my age, but I was not about to take any chances. I do not remember her name. I was, however, aware of how the Army would deal with me if I were apprehended being involved with a minor.

The night before graduation from the Army Air Corps School I went to St. Louis again to celebrate graduation. I again drank too much. Late that night I started looking for a ride back to camp. I found a civilian in a bar that said he would get me back to camp. He borrowed a fellow's car to give me a ride back to camp.

On our trip back to camp he picked up two more soldiers who were also hitchhiking back to camp. It was about two O'clock in the morning when our car started acting up. Although we had no lights and the car would only travel about fifteen miles per hour, the driver continued down the road toward Scott Field. I was riding in the front seat with the driver. I had a bottle of Coke spiked with a little whiskey in my hand. We went over a hill and were just starting down the other side when a car came over the hill behind us and crashed into the rear of our car. We careened off the road and as we came to a stop, I felt the car go up at an angle almost onto one side, then drop back down on all four wheels. I knew we had nearly rolled over onto the side of the car. I glanced around at the other three people in our car. They all looked unconscious to me. I also noticed that I had hit the glove compartment door in front of me and had knocked the clock out of it during the crash. In those days some cars had a small clock in the glove compartment door. I couldn't feel any pain but I did notice that there was fluid running down my face. I thought that I was bleeding but couldn't tell for sure because it was dark. I got out of the car and looked at the car that had hit us. It was still sitting on the highway right where it had hit us. Steam was pouring out of the engine and all occupants of that car were either unconscious or moaning. I noticed that one person had broken the windshield. I decided to leave the scene and walk back to the base. About that time, a farmer came running up the road with a flashlight and ordered me to get back up on that hill and flag traffic with the flashlight. I asked him if I was bleeding and he said that I was not. I guess it must have been Coke spilled on me. I stood at the crest of the hill flagging down any oncoming traffic. After a while the Military Police vehicles and the ambulances arrived. I was taken straight to the guardhouse in a military police vehicle and questioned by the Duty Officer. I was unable to help them because I did not know anyone in either car. They then took me to the base hospital where I was checked and told to go to the barracks. I was awakened early in the morning in time to go to school for the Class Graduation Ceremonies. I couldn't raise my head off the pillow to get up alone. My neck was so stiff, I had to have help getting out of bed.

I managed to get ready and made it to school. I was honored at the graduation ceremony for being on of just a few people in the class who had achieved copying 30 words per minute of the International Morse Code. I received my Diploma and my Travel Orders transferring me to Patterson Field, Ohio for assignment to a line organization known as AACS (Airways and Air

Communications Service). I had been granted a 30-day leave of absence. I made it home that same day. I never heard from anyone concerning that automobile accident again. At the end of my leave of absence in Wisconsin, I hitchhiked to my new assignment at Patterson Field, Ohio. I arrived at the base early in the morning on December 7th, 1941. I was issued bedding and was assigned a bed in the open area of the barracks and went to bed. Later that day, I as awakened to the news that the Japanese had attacked Pearl Harbor. I enjoyed my stay at Patterson Field where I was to receive further training as an operator in the reception and transmission of live traffic via radio over the Communications CW Network. I met many new people during my assignment. Many exciting things were happening because of the fact that we were at war with the Japanese and by now the Germans over in Europe. Many of the old timers in AACS were being transferred overseas. A very large group was forming for transfer to Africa to establish new bases. I volunteered for transfer to Africa but was turned down.

Four months after my arrival at Patterson Field, I became involved with a married woman who lived in Fairfield, Ohio. This fact became general knowledge within the Communications Squadron and I was ordered to stop this involvement. I ignored the order. Within a very short time, I was transferred, which was the Army's way of handling the situation. I was told on a day in early May 1942 that I would depart for my new assignment at Connellsville, Pennsylvania.

DEPARTMENT OF COMMUNICATIONS
THE AIR CORPS TECHNICAL SCHOOL
SCOTT FIELD, ILL.

TO ALL WHOM IT MAY CONCERN

GREETINGS;

This is to certify that Pvt. James E. Parenteau *a student in Class* 23C RADIO OPERATORS and MECHANICS COURSE *has attained a* CODE *speed of* 30 *words per minute.*

In witness thereof we have affixed our signatures this 21st *day of* November *194*1

D.E. Sherman

D.E. Sherman, 2nd Lt., A. C.
SUPERVISOR
RADIO OPERATING DIVISION

T.M. Hetherington

T.M. HETHERINGTON, Major, A.C.
DIRECTOR

---------- 1941 ------------
SPECIAL AWARD FROM TRAINING
CLASS FOR PASSING A CW TEST
AT 30 WORDS PER MINUTE.
JIM PARENTEAU US ARMY

Working the radio equipment at the Connellsville airport.

CHAPTER 4

MEETING THE LOVE OF MY LIFE

The day I left Dayton, Ohio we were having a late spring snowstorm. I traveled by train in May 1942 to Connellsville, Pennsylvania. The snowstorm had hit Connellsville too but in a short time spring was in full bloom.

I was really impressed with Connellsville. I found out that there were only about 8 or 10 soldiers assigned to the Connellsville Airport. Our detachment operated and maintained a Radio Range Station, a Communications Relay Station, and Communications transmitters and receivers. Our mission was to relay messages between Patterson Field and Bolling Field located in Washington D.C. We had no barracks so we were allowed to live in town. We lived in boarding houses in the city of Connellsville and received extra pay for meals and quarters. What a plush assignment. One of the fringe benefits was that we were allowed to go to a civilian dentist and the government would pay the bill.

I was having trouble with my two front teeth that had been loosened in the street fight before coming into the service. I also had many cavities. I took advantage of the free dental privileges. It was there that I met Hazel Cokenour. She was the dental assistant and receptionist. I dated Hazel for a while.

One evening I was to pick Hazel up at her house. I was running a bit early. I decided to take a walk around the block where I lived to pass away the time. As I was walking I heard an automobile crash and a horn stuck. I quickly went to see the accident. There were three cars in the accident. I noticed that there was a good-looking girl, about my age, in the center car. I helped her out of the car but someone whisked her away before I got her name. I was interested enough to run back to my boarding house and get my camera to take some pictures of the accident. I asked around to get the girl's name and address. Her name was Winifred (Winnie) McCairns. I made plans to have the pictures developed and thereby have an excuse to get to know her.

I did get the opportunity to visit her and show her the pictures. I learned that she was engaged to be married. I also found out that her father owned a foundry in town. When I saw where she lived and the foundry I knew that she was from a different class of people than me. I knew what my background was and decided to get out of this situation. I had a friend in the service at the Airport to whom I introduced her. I hoped they would hit it off. What I didn't know was that this lady was thinking of breaking up with the man she was engaged to and had made up her mind that she was going to marry me.

Winnie had given me a recent snapshot taken of her while at Atlantic City, New Jersey. One evening shortly thereafter, while I was working the midnight shift at the Communications Center at the Airport, I spent most of the night looking at the snapshot of her. I believe that I fell in love with Winnie that night. The next morning, I went after that girl.

We had a beautiful courtship. I was a very happy person in my new assignment in beautiful Pennsylvania. I continually told her that I wanted to marry her. She finally agreed to marry me. I wanted my father and mother to meet her. They made a railroad trip to Connellsville. I will never forget my father's reaction to meeting her. Winnie was a petite girl who weighed 98 pounds and was 5' 2". My father said "Jim, couldn't you find a healthier girl?"

We believed that we couldn't tell Winnie's parents that we were going to be married. We decided to elope. Our plans were to travel to Oakland, Maryland to be married. Money was in short supply in those days. We decided that when the paychecks arrived in June, I would call Winnie and we would leave the following day after work. In the meantime, I found a beautiful apartment in a private home on Eighth Street in Connellsville, about four blocks from Winnie's home. Winnie purchased a white dress and secretly moved many of her belongings into my apartment. When the checks arrived in the mail at Connellsville Airport in June of 1942, I told everyone there that I was eloping with Winnie McCairns the next day.

Late that night, about 2 AM, Winnie's sister Isabel came to my boarding house and told me that Bill Putt, a Civilian Guard at the Airport, had told Bud Miller (Isabel's husband) the news of our elopement. She also told me that while Bud and Winnie's father were drinking that evening, Bud had told him that we were gong to elope the next day. Her father was going to stop us from eloping.

That morning at about 5AM the landlady knocked on my door again and told me that there was a Mrs. McCairns there to see me. I dressed and went outside and sat in the car with Winnie's mother. She said that Mr. McCairns had learned that I was going to elope with their daughter and that she was not of legal age. She told me that the Connellsville police would arrest me if I tried to elope with her daughter. I asked her when Winnie would be of legal age and she replied that she would be 21 on the 18th of August. I told her that Winnie was not pregnant and that we would just wait until August and then we would elope. I called Winnie later in the morning and told her of the change in plans.

I decided to get even with Bill Putt for blowing the whistle on my elopement plans. I knew that Bill, a Civil Service guard, had the habit of sleeping on guard duty. I asked a few of the soldiers at the airport to come along and be witnesses for me. We went to the airport late that night and I woke Bill and told him that I would report him in the morning. I reported the incident to Mr. Putt's boss the next morning. I was told that even though I had witnesses, I did not have a case since I did not take his gun away from him. I could have done that easily because when Bill would lie down to go to sleep he would hang his gun in the unlocked wall locker next to the bed. I knew that they believed me but that they would not prosecute him. I considered more drastic measures but decided that they were too drastic.

I was not allowed to pick Winnie up at her house. We made arrangements to meet and continued to date. I had previously located an apartment in a private home just a few blocks from her house. The apartment was on the second floor and could be reached by climbing steps built on the outside of the house to the second floor entrance. We nicknamed it “Lover's Leap” because of the high steps to our apartment.

We decided that we would play it cool for a month until our next paycheck and then make another attempt to go to Maryland

and be married. In the meantime every so often Winnie would wear her white outfit, which she planned to wear for the wedding, when going out for the evening with me. She would come down the stairs in her home singing, "Here comes the bride." Winnie also carried small amounts of clothing when she left the house. This allowed us to build up a supply of clothing at my apartment. We also set up a signal that we would use in our conversations to tell her that my check had arrived and our plans were put into action for our wedding to take place that evening.

JAMES E. PARENTEAU
BORN 4 NOVEMBER 1921
SUPERIOR, WISCONSIN
PART 2

CHAPTER 5

WEDDING BELLS

On 2 July 1942, I received my paycheck. I called Winnie and gave her the signal. We had made arrangements with S/Sgt.[1] Tom Cline and Delores Hankle to be best man and bridesmaid. I called him and we were all to meet at my apartment after dinner. Winnie arrived at my apartment in her white outfit, Tom and Delores arrived to provide transportation, and we took off for Oakland, Maryland. I kept watching out the rear window to be sure that neither Winnie's parents nor the Pennsylvania State Police were coming after us. I relaxed after we left Pennsylvania and were in Maryland.

We stopped at Deep Creek Lake, Maryland and rented a cabin for four days and drove on to Oakland, Maryland. We drove around trying to find a Methodist Church for a while with no luck. We decided to stop at the priest's home next to a Catholic Church and ask for directions. I went up and rang the doorbell. The priest answered the door and I said "Father, would you give me directions to the Methodist Church?" I immediately figured he knew that I was Catholic and looking for a place to get married. However, he didn't have a problem with telling me how to get to the church.

We met The Reverend Minor Sprague of St. Paul's Methodist Church and were married in the parsonage at 10:00 PM on 2 July 1942. It obviously was a beautiful wedding since our marriage remains a happy marriage as I write this in 1995, nearly fifty-three years later. As we left the parsonage we located a Western Union facility at the railroad station and sent a telegram to Winnie's mother and father to advise them that we were just

[1] Staff Sergeant, one pay grade above Sergeant

married. We then passed an amusement park and decided to stop and visit. Winnie and I decided to take a ride on the Ferris wheel. After an extended ride we finally figured out that the operator of the Ferris wheel was letting everyone off and picking up new passengers to replace everyone but us. After a while we finally convinced him to let us off. Tom and Delores dropped us off at the Deep Creek Lake cabin and returned to Pennsylvania.

Winnie and I spent a beautiful four days at Deep Creek Lake. We did not have a car and planned to take a bus back to Connellsville, Pennsylvania. However, we met two young men at the lake who were driving back to the Connellsville area on the same day we had planned to travel. They gave us a ride back to our apartment in Connellsville.

When I returned to work I found out that while I was away I had been promoted to Sergeant effective 1 July 1942. I also found out that the following Monday I was on orders to go to Scott Field to attend Advanced Radio Mechanic School. The course was a six-week course and I would return to Connellsville Airport at the completion of the course. Winnie was able to come and spend a weekend with me about midway through the course. I returned to Connellsville in mid August.

In September I was working the day shift transmitting messages back and forth over the network. I received a call from Wright Patterson on the radio network. The other operator asked me who I was and I told him. He transmitted the message to me and as I copied the message I found out that it concerned me. It was my permanent change of station orders transferring me to a staging area in Great Falls, Montana for further assignment to Destination Unknown. As I departed by rail to Great Falls Winnie accompanied me as far as Cincinnati, Ohio. She waved goodbye to me there and she returned to Connellsville. That was one of the saddest days of our lives. We had spent only a short time together as a married couple. Those were beautiful days but as we parted in Cincinnati that day neither one of us knew when or if we would ever see each other again. I was off to the war.

Wedding Picture
Jim and Winnie Parenteau

CHAPTER 6

A MILITARY WIFE

I arrived in Great Falls, Montana and was advised that the organization to which I was assigned had not yet been formed. I was quartered in the YMCA in Great Falls and was told the unit would be activated in about two weeks. Shortly thereafter we were told that the unit was activated and where to report. We were briefed that the new Army Air Corps Communications Unit was being established to operate and manage communications support to the top secret route whose mission was to build airports at The Pas, Alberta, Canada and Churchill, Canada (Hudson Bay Territory) to hook up with Goose Bay, Canada, a base called BW-1 (Bluie West One) in Greenland, and Iceland to provide a means of flying pursuit fighter planes to England. We would receive special training to aid us in providing the communication support for this new route. We were sworn to secrecy and cautioned not to reveal our destination upon being advised as to which unit we would ultimately be assigned. Everything was TOP Secret.

I was very happy to find out that I would not be leaving North America for the present time. I had believed that we were probably being staged for shipment to the Pacific Area. I considered myself well off to be in this organization. We received our training and I was a member of the first five enlisted personnel in our organization to depart from the USA for our assigned Top Secret destination: The Pas, Manitoba, Canada. At that time there were no Commissioned Officers from our unit assigned to that destination. S/Sgt. Campbell was our NCOIC[2]. I was a S/Sgt. at that time but was outranked by S/Sgt. Campbell. I was thus second in command. We departed Great Falls on November 4th, 1942 (my 21st birthday). We arrived at The Pas, our destination, on November 5th. We were met at the railroad station and transported twenty-five miles from The Pas to the site of our new base. We found a U.S. Army Engineer Battalion at the base that was engaged in building barracks, and all other base developments needed to support the

---

[2] Non-Commissioned Officer In Charge

operation. The building project was in its very initial stages. Civilian contractors were building transmitter sites, radio range sites, etc. Initially, we were used primarily for guard duty after our arrival.

Since we were a small Army Air Corps unit assigned to the base, we soon found that we were given special privileges that the Army Engineers did not get. We were not subject to Kitchen Police details; the engineers did all the K.P. duties. Also, engineers were allowed to visit The Pas (25 miles away) only once a week, had to be accompanied by military police and had a curfew of 10:00 PM. Air Corps personnel were allowed to visit The Pas at any time we were off duty. Transportation was a problem that was overcome by hitchhiking during the day and taking a taxicab at other times. If not on duty we could stay in town overnight. There was one hotel and rooms were reasonable. These differences in treatment were naturally very obvious on this small base and a source of many hard feelings between the engineers and the Air Corps unit during the entire assignment.

Shortly after my arrival at the base, I got an idea. Suppose that I could find a place to rent in The Pas. Although my mail was censored, perhaps I could get away with making a long distance phone call to Winnie in Pennsylvania. I could tell her where I was and ask her to get on a train and come north to visit for a while. She would have to use her maiden name so that no one could find out that she was my wife. I knew that I would be in serious trouble if the authorities were to discover what I had done; but if I was not found out, I could see Winnie again. Should I take the risk?

I decided to take the risk. The very next time I went to town my mission was clear. I thought about my plan. Who could I approach to safely ask questions about finding a place to rent? I believed that my best opportunity would be to become friends with the railroad telegrapher. I had been very active in Wisconsin as a student learning railroad telegraph work. I went straight to the depot. I talked to the telegrapher for a few minutes and told him I would like to talk to him when he got off duty. He agreed and told me he was off at midnight. I sat around the depot waiting for midnight to arrive. In the meantime, the depot janitor and I got to talking. He was very friendly. In talking to him, I said I was interested in finding a small house for rent. He said he knew of one that was just a few houses away from his house. He said he was going to go home for lunch at 10:00 PM. I could accompany him and he would show me where the house was located.

I went with him to his house. He invited me to have a late midnight snack with he and his wife, which I did. After finishing eating, he invited me to sleep on the couch that night if I desired. He had to go back to work until 8:00 AM. I slept in his house that night, a total stranger, with his wife and two small children the only others in the house. The next morning when he got off work, he took me over to a little house nearby and showed me around and told me that I could rent the house for $10.00 per month; eight dollars for the house and two dollars for the furniture. I said it was a deal. I asked him to make the arrangements for me and went back to the base.

I got acquainted with him and his family. I asked them to pose as Winnie's aunt and uncle and write a letter to her and ask her to come and visit them. When Winnie got their letter, she made arrangements to leave Pennsylvania and depart for The Pas, Manitoba, Canada; a little town just about 500 miles north of Winnipeg, Alberta, Canada. In the meantime, I spent a lot of time in that house. I repainted the inside of the house. The house had no heater, just a small cook stove that was inadequate for heating the house properly. There was no running water and no toilet facilities except an outside privy. Making preparation for the trip from Pennsylvania to The Pas was no ordinary feat. Winnie's father was not in favor of her going. He talked her out of using her maiden name in an effort to protect her from unknown problems for falsifying her identification. I had told only my best friend at the base what I was doing. He promised to tell no one. I then spread the word at my unit that I was living with a woman whose husband worked on the railroad and was out of town most of the time. I needed this cover for being away from the base so much. Finally, I got the word through Winnie's new aunt and uncle that Winnie would arrive at The Pas on December 24th 1942. Her new aunt would meet the train and bring Winnie to our new house. I could not take the chance to meet her at the station. After dark on December 24, I heard the train come into town, I stood at the window and watched hoping that Winnie and her new aunt would get together at the station. After what seemed like an eternity, I saw Winnie and Jean Stephenson come walking home from the depot. We had made my scheme work, for the moment at least.

After Winnie's arrival we spent most of our time together in that house. She had to stay there alone when I had to work – but I would come home any time that I had enough hours to visit her and get back to the base. Our first rule was that we would never be seen leaving that house together. I would leave and then I would meet her somewhere shortly thereafter. One night we decided to go to a restaurant in town. There were only two restaurants in the town. We were sitting having our dinner and I looked up and saw S/Sgt. Campbell come into the restaurant. I told her we are in trouble now. I kept Winnie's picture on my bedside at the base. Winnie hurriedly mussed up her hair and tried to imitate speaking like a Canadian as Sgt. Campbell walked right over to our booth and sat down. One of the things Winnie did to throw him off was that she dropped a penny on the floor and said, "Oh, I just dropped one of my coppers." The Canadians always called their pennies "Coppers." We breathed a sigh of relief when Sgt. Campbell left our booth and went on his way. Sgt. Campbell never suspected anything and never even mentioned the occasion again. We hurried and got out of there as fast as we could. Another time we decided to go to a movie theater. We went in separately and sat together. When we left the theater Winnie said "I have to use the ladies room." I waited in the hall nearby and while I was standing there a lady usher in the theater came up to me and said, "I know what you two are doing." I just turned and walked away. I didn't know if she really knew what was going on, or if perhaps she had heard the rumor that I was spreading about living with a railroad man's wife.

Occasionally an Army bus would be making a trip to town. We knew of the trip so I decided to go back to the base when it left town. Winnie walked down to the bus with me. I said goodbye and loaded onto the bus. I saw Sgt. Silk on the bus so I sat down beside him. He was in our organization and lived in the same barracks as I. on the trip to the base he had a long talk to me and told me that I was ruining that lady's life. He said that she looked very sad. He told me that I should break off that relationship. Three years later, Winnie and I met Sgt. Silk while we were stationed in the town of

Fort St. John, British Columbia, Canada. He was stopping overnight on a return trip to the U.S. We invited him to our house and told him the real story of our experience in The Pas. He really enjoyed knowing the truth of what we had done.

One time when Winnie had been alone for a spell while I had to work, she went over and visited her newly acquired Aunt Jean. When she returned home that evening, she walked into the house and found an intoxicated Indian sitting in the middle of our kitchen table. She managed to get him out of the house without a major problem. We had heard that there was a bad band of Indians – believe it or not – they were known as the Parenteau tribe. I really did not make that up. I never bothered to try and find out if that was true or not. I really did not want to know. We were told that those Indians lived just outside of town. Perhaps we were related. Strange coincidence.

We had neither running water nor a well at The Pas. There was one well in the town and the owner of the well had a horse and wagon to haul the water to customers in the town. We had a metal storage tank in the kitchen in which to store the water. When it started getting low we would have to hang the water sign on the outside of the kitchen door and the water man would deliver water to fill the storage tank. He carried two buckets at a time from the wagon to our storage tank. The going price was five cents a bucket. Once when he was delivering the water, he had snow on his boots and when he hit the linoleum floor in the kitchen he slipped and fell, spilling both buckets onto the kitchen floor. Living this life was full of surprises.

I mentioned before that the house had no heater, just a small cook stove. There was a load of wood sawed up in our yard. We used the wood to cook our meals. At night when we went to bed we put three little pieces of wood onto the fire – that was all it would hold. In about forty-five minutes the stove would burn out. The rest of the night we had no heat until we awakened the next morning. During January the temperature reached 50 below zero Fahrenheit and stayed that cold for two weeks. We had a canteen of water that we kept on the floor next to the bed. Every morning that water was frozen solid. Also, remember that we had no inside toilet. That was another major problem.

I made trips back and forth at every opportunity that I had while Winnie was there. On many trips, I hitched a ride where I had to sit in the open bed of a pickup truck or in the open back of a military truck. The 25-mile trip on those narrow backcountry dirt roads took a long time. I had a fur lined military Gaffney Flying Suit. By the time I got home the parka hood had a buildup of frost that covered my whole face. On one trip I received a ride in the back of a military truck that was loaded with giant spools of communications cable. We went off the road and the truck rolled over on its side. When it did, the entire load shifted and to my good fortune the spools fell all around and above me but did not hit any part of my body. The officer in the cab got out and yelled, "Are you all right?" I advised him that I was okay. They had to very carefully unload the truck of all the spools and get it back on its wheels before we were able to complete the trip.

When the temperature finally warmed up to a reasonable thirty degrees below zero we were going to go and visit the Mallards one evening. They owned the grocery store where Winnie bought her groceries. They were the only other family that knew we were married and that Winnie was visiting from the USA. Winnie got ready to go and I noticed that she had a pair of anklets on her legs. I asked her to please put a pair of stockings on because it was still very cold out. She refused to dress warmer. I told her that if she got sick I would ship her back to the States. She did get a cold the next day but as you guessed, she was not shipped back to the States.

There is a difference of opinion on this next event. Winnie says it happened later during our assignment at Fort St. John, British Columbia. I say it happened at The Pas. Either way, this is what happened. It was dark outside; I don't remember what time it was. One of us went outside the house for whatever reason and came flying back into the house shouting, "Come outside and see what is happening!" We looked up and the whole sky was flashing in full color. At first it appeared to be a shiny fog full of every color in the rainbow. I think we thought it was the end of the world. The rolling fog was just a little bit higher than the buildings. The colors kept changing. Finally, the lights grew higher and higher and faded away. The next day we found out from the Stephenson's that it was the Aurora Borealis. What a beautiful sight! Living in Superior,

Wisconsin until my teen years I had seen the Aurora Borealis many times. However, in Wisconsin they were always very far away, just above the horizon, and they were always just a dim white light across the sky.

We lived very happily in our little house rental for about six weeks. Then one day the word was circulated that Lieutenant Geodarno, the Signal Corp Officer-In-Charge was in big trouble. He had told his wife where he was and had her come to the town of Flin Flon[3] to visit him. She was living in Flin Flon; he did not keep it a secret and somehow the information had reached the Base Commander. Immediately, the Base Commander had sworn her to secrecy and shipped her back to the U.S. The rumor was that the Lieutenant might be Court Martialed. I immediately went to town and Winnie packed and left The Pas on the train the next day for her return trip to Pennsylvania. We were later to learn that the Lieutenant was not Court Martialed, but that he would remain in his present rank for the remainder of his military service. His military records were somehow annotated with that form of punishment. I never knew whether that punishment was possible or not. We never heard any more about the situation.

One last comment about The Pas... Winnie returned to Pennsylvania in good health and expecting our first child. I returned to barracks life and no one was the wiser. Not one word leaked out about her trip to The Pas.

Three months later, in May 1943, I was fortunate to be granted two weeks military furlough. I met Winnie at the railroad station in Pittsburg, Pennsylvania. We stayed in a nice hotel in Pittsburg for a few days and then returned to her father's home in Connellsville for the remainder of the visit. Winnie and I had taken a wonderful visit.

I returned to The Pas via Superior, Wisconsin where I visited with my parents for a couple of days.

Within a month or two thereafter the military aborted the entire project of building the airports and the idea of flying pursuit

---

[3] A copper mining town about 60 or 75 miles north of The Pas

aircraft via the proposed route. That fantastic assignment would terminate immediately and all personnel would be transferred to various assignments. Again, we had no idea where we would end up. I was soon to receive my orders transferring me to a Communications Group at Edmonton, Alberta, Canada for further shipment to Alaska. There were enough troops going that route to make up a trop train. I was assigned duty as NCO in charge of the troop train. There were several officers also being transferred along with us on that troop train. I had very few duties on the train, but I did have to sign the voucher for the tickets used to transport the troops.

We spent only a few days at Edmonton and were transported to Anchorage, Alaska. At Anchorage we lived in a tent city awaiting further orders. We had to stand inspections and performed work details there. Somehow, I was able to see someone about my assignment. I do not remember the details. I did request that I be assigned to Ladd AFB[4] in Fairbanks, Alaska. I knew it was a big city and the best place in Alaska to be stationed. I never received an answer until the day that the orders were issued. Luckily, I was assigned to Fairbanks, Alaska. My friends were assigned all over the Aleutian Islands, or to outposts at Galena, Nome, or Point Barrow. I was the only one I knew who received an assignment to Fairbanks. Obviously it must occasionally pay to ask.

I enjoyed my assignment at Ladd AFB. We had heated underground passageways to walk to work and to other places on the base. However, about two months after my arrival at Ladd AFB, I went to town one evening. I was drinking at a bar until about a quarter to ten. The bartender told me that there was a curfew and that if I purchased a few drinks before curfew I could stay and drink them. One just couldn't buy a drink after curfew. I bought a few and they set them up on the bar in front of me. A short time later at 10:00 PM two military police came into the bar and said "Everyone out. The curfew is in effect." I put up an argument and was carted off with an M.P. on each arm. I was taken to the guardhouse at the base and locked up for the night to sober up. I was then given Company Punishment of one week hard labor.

---

[4] Air Force Base

I served that week of hard labor as a T/Sgt.,[5] digging ditches in the frozen tundra. I was very surprised that I did not get a reduction in rank. Almost immediately after I served my punishment, I was called in to the Orderly Room and advised that I was being transferred to Nome, Alaska; which is on the Siberian Peninsula. My big mouth had gotten me into deep trouble.

I departed for Nome. In Nome we did not have any nice barracks. We lived in Quonset huts. We didn't have running water or latrines in the Quonset huts. We had to walk about four blocks to an outdoor latrine with no running water. In Nome we walked outdoors everywhere we went. The city of Nome was about five miles or so from the base. The population of Nome consisted mostly of Eskimo families. The main street in Nome was about four blocks long with only one restaurant.

Nome was not the worst place in Alaska. There were smaller outposts. There were rumors that the Japanese had plans to land troops at Nome and gain a foothold on the mainland of Alaska. They had already landed Japanese military forces in the Aleutian Islands. However, history has recorded that they never attempted a landing at Nome.

Our mission at Nome was to provide communications support to aircraft flying to Russia under the USA Lend Lease Program. American pilots flew the aircraft, B-25's, A-29's, P-39's, P-51's and P-53's as far as Fairbanks. Russian flight crews then manned the aircraft to fly them to Galena, Alaska and on to Nome for refueling before taking off for Russia. At Nome US Air Corps and Russian communications personnel operated our control tower and radio operations for voice and C.W.[6] jointly. I was a C.W. Operator and worked shifts around the clock. We were always short of personnel to the extent that we often worked 12 hours on and 12 hours off with no days off. That was not really a hardship because there was nothing to do if you had a day off. There were no leaves of absence other than an occasional leave of absence to attend a close family funeral.

---

[5] Technical (or Tech) Sergeant, one pay grade above Staff Sergeant

[6] Continuous Wave, or International Morse Code

It was very enjoyable working with and getting to know the Russian military personnel. I learned some Russian phrases but had a close military friend who was also a radio operator. His name was Alex Atanasoff from Hershey, Pennsylvania. Alex could converse with the Russians.

One day Alex and I were talking and I told him that I would like to get a picture of me in a Russian officer's uniform. The one Russian officer we knew always hung his officer's blouse and hat on the same rack we did, right next to the exit door. The door was about eight feet behind the C.W. operators' operating positions. We decided to give it a try. I picked up the blouse and hat, stepped out onto the entrance and Alex took my picture a couple of times. I hung the coat and hat up on the rack and nothing was said. The next day I was called in to the Russian interpreter's office. I was verbally reprimanded for my inappropriate behavior and directed to turn over the film in my camera. I was also told to apologize to the officer, which I did with Alex's help. I never saw that film again nor did I ever hear any more about the incident. I suppose the Russian had seen what happened because I was never to learn how the incident got reported.

I don't know where the Russian enlisted personnel lived. We did associate with them I have a picture of me and another American C.W. operator ice-skating with two of the Russian airmen on a pond at Nome.

Outside the quarters in Canada

CHAPTER 7

FATHERHOOD

Our first child, Bonnie Ann was born on September 26, 1943. When I received the letter from Winnie's mother Mabel telling me that Bonnie was born I bought a fifth of liquor and Ray Verlinde and I went to Nome for a dinner of Caribou steak. We put the fifth on the table and were having a dinner. The next thing I remembered was waking up in the Military Police station. Ray was on the floor and one of the police was kicking him. I stood up and took a swing at one of the policemen but fortunately for me I missed him altogether. When we sobered up somewhat, the MP's drove us back to the base and dropped us off at the building where we worked. Ray went on back to the Quonset hut ahead of me. It was about 1:00 AM when I started back to the hut. I had about two blocks to walk. I obviously passed out en-route. I awakened the following morning and I was in my bed. I was stiff and found it difficult to move. I later learned that one of the men in one of the Quonset huts had gone up to the latrine during the night and found me lying in the snow between the latrine and the huts. He somehow got me back to the hut area and found out where I lived and got me to my bed. I had no memory of anything after I left the work area except for a brief period of time when I was trying to crawl over the snowdrifts and I was having a very difficult time. I obviously did not make it on my own. It was a cold night and I am sure that if that airman had not found me I would have frozen to death. A few days later, I heard that one of the Base Chaplains was found frozen to death just about twenty yards from his quarters. They did not find him until morning. What the circumstances were in his case I never knew.

In about the month of February 1943 our Group Commanding Officer from Edmonton, Canada visited us in Nome. A meeting was held in the station office. The commander briefed us and he answered whatever questions he was asked. As the meeting broke up, the commander advised us that he would be available on the following day if anyone had any problem they would like to speak to him about privately. I decided that I would like to have a talk with him. I don't remember whether I was the only one who went to see him or not, but I do remember that we had a nice talk. I told him my problem was that I had a wife and a new daughter in the States whom I had never seen. I would certainly appreciate it if I could get transferred to Edmonton or somewhere south where I could get to see them. He said he would look into the matter. I didn't even hear from him again. However, about three months later our Officer in Charge called me in to advise me that he had just received orders for my transfer to Prince George, British Columbia, Canada. Although our mail was censored, I went right down to the Nome Western Union Office and sent a telegram to Winnie in Pennsylvania. It read: "TRANSFERRED TO PRINCE GEORGE BRITISH COLUMBIA STOP NEED A COOK. SIGNED JIM."

About two weeks later I arrived in Prince George. I could not find a place for us to live but did find that I could rent a hotel room by the month. I could talk to Winnie on the telephone from Prince George. There was neither any censorship nor any objection to our calling the US from there. Late one night shortly thereafter (I believe it was May 1944) she and Bonnie Ann arrived at Prince George, British Columbia. The hotel was located about a half block from the depot. I met the train and was introduced to our daughter, Bonnie Ann, who was about 8 months old. I had obtained a crib and when Winnie put Bonnie Ann in the crib, Bonnie cried. She had a good set of lungs. I

With Winnie & Bonnie in Canada

was never allowed to forget my reaction. I said "Pick it up, it's going to wake up everyone in the hotel."

We lived in the hotel for one month. We ate all of our meals in the hotels very small dining room. It was a very nice life style, however, we could see that we were spending much more than we were making. We had to find a new place within our means or else. The only place we could find to live was a tent-top cabin on the Prince George River. There were other families living in the tent-top places and there were also a few small wooden cabins. We moved into one of the tent-top cabins. It was a very uncomfortable place to live, but we were together. Many mornings when one awakened and dressed, the clothes were very damp. During our stay in that place Bonnie appeared to come down with whooping cough. We were finally able to move into one of the wooden cabins which were much more comfortable. The cabin had only one small room.

In August 1944 we were notified that the U.S. facilities at Prince George were closing. I received orders transferring me to Fort St. John, British Columbia, Canada. We traveled via rail to Edmonton, Alberta, Canada. In Edmonton we visited a day or two with Ray Verlindi, my friend from Nome, Alaska who had since married a native of Alaska. He was now stationed at Edmonton. Then Winnie, Bonnie Ann and I traveled by rail to Dawson Creek, British Columbia. Dawson Creek was the end of the rail lines. We traveled by auto the remaining forty miles up the Alaskan Highway to Fort St. John, British Columbia. Fort St. John was a small town with dirt roads located about ten miles from the U.S. Base of the same name. We located a small one-room house with no running water. The water supply for the whole town came from one well in town. Again, we were back to buying water by the bucket. We had a container for storing our water. Shortly thereafter, I was very fortunate to obtain a larger house. It had a kitchen, a living room, a normal sized bedroom and a small bedroom for Bonnie Ann. It also had a room with a chemical toilet, and that was our bathroom. We ordered living room furniture from Edmonton and had it shipped to our new home. One day on the way to work I saw a metal object that looked like a horse trough stored against a building. I was able to buy it and we put it in our bathroom. I was the only person we knew among the American soldiers living in Ft.

St. John who had a bathtub. You had to heat the water and pour it into the tub and then carry the water outside and pour it out. Some of our friends' wives' would come over to our house occasionally to take a bath.

Our mission in Ft. St. John was to provide an airstrip where planes from the U.S. would stop off to refuel on their route to Fairbanks and ultimately to Russia via Nome, Alaska again under the lend lease program. While we were together at Ft. St. John, the war ended in Europe (V.E. Day). We remained in Ft. St. John until near to the end of the war with the Japanese. When the war was nearing the end of World War II, the military came out with a point system. If you had enough points you could either stay in the service where you were stationed or you could sign a paper saying you wanted to get out of the service and be transferred back to the States and be discharged from the service. We thought about it and decided that we would take a chance and sign the paper and go back to the States. When we got back we would say we had changed our minds and wanted to stay in the service. We hoped that would work because we were very happy in the service.

On 30 June 1945 I received my orders transferring me to Sheppard Field, Wichita Falls, Texas on project "Readjustment." I was allowed a delay en-route that enabled me to stop in Spooner, Wisconsin where we visited my family. While there, we decided to leave Bonnie Ann with my mother while Winnie and I went to Texas for a week. After a week in Texas, Winnie and I returned to Wisconsin, picked up Bonnie and traveled to East Orange, New Jersey to visit her family. During those two weeks the Japanese surrendered and V-J Day was celebrated. At the end of the two weeks I returned to Sheppard AFB.

In Texas I went in to see the Personnel Officer and told him that I did not want to leave the service. He informed me that I had no choice. Once I signed that paper I had to be discharged in accordance with the regulations. I received orders transferring me to Fort Dix, New Jersey for discharge from the Army Air Force. I was discharged form the service on 1 September 1945 with the rank of Technical Sergeant. When I walked away from the Officer who discharged me I was asked by a recruiting Officer if I would like to re-enlist. I said "No thanks, I am out of the service now and I do not plan to re-enlist."

I went directly to Frank and Mabel McCairns apartment where Winnie and Bonnie Ann were staying to start my new life as a civilian. We were lucky to be able to locate a third floor apartment within a very short time. The apartment was only about six blocks from Frank and Mabel's apartment in East Orange, New Jersey.

JAMES E. PARENTEAU
BORN 4 NOVEMBER 1921
SUPERIOR, WISCONSIN
PART 3

CHAPTER 8

POST-WORLD WAR II

My first priority was to find a job in New Jersey. Prior to leaving the service, while visiting in New Jersey, I had gone to the Pennsylvania Railroad offices in Brooklyn, New York and inquired about employment. I had been interviewed for a job as a telegrapher on the Pennsylvania Railroad. I had been favorably considered and was advised that there were many vacancies. I could not take a job at that point because I was still in the service. I told them that I was to be discharged shortly and that I would contact them when I was free to accept employment.

After my discharge at Ft. Dix on 1 September, I returned to Brooklyn to discuss employment with the Pennsylvania Railroad. They advised me that the situation had changed drastically since the War had ended in August. Innumerable prior employees were returning from World War II. They had been promised when they entered the service that at the end of the war their jobs would be available to them. All hiring of anyone who had not previously worked for the Pennsylvania Railroad was frozen indefinitely.

This was not good news for me. I searched for employment for two weeks and was really concerned that I would not be able to find employment. In the third week I had an interview with the Western Union Telegraph Company and was offered a job in the Western Union Office on Main Street in East Orange, New Jersey. I would start as a counter clerk and telephone operator accepting telegrams. My starting salary would be fifty cents an hour. I accepted the job. I could hardly support a family on 40 hours a week, which equated to $20.00 a week. Therefore, I immediately took advantage of every opportunity to work overtime that arose with Western Union. I worked my regular shift of 40 hours a week and as much as 40 hours overtime when I had the opportunity. Winnie and I did not make any friends in New Jersey. The people we met seemed to us to be very unhappy people. It wasn't unusual for us to get the urge to leave New Jersey every time we heard the lonesome whistle of a passenger train in the night.

I wasn't there very long when the employees of Western Union went on a strike. I was very happy that the strike lasted only a very short time. The employees settled for a 5-cent an hour rise in pay. That didn't make much of a difference in my salary.

I soon had the opportunity to work overtime as a night office manager of the Western Union office in Mountclair, New Jersey. However, I received the same basic salary of fifty-five cents an hour at time and a half even though I was a night manager.

In April of 1946, just eight months after my discharge from the service, we received a letter from my old Air Force Headquarters Unit advising me that they would like me to re-enlist in the Air Force. They offered me the rank of Permanent Staff Sergeant. All promotions in the enlisted ranks had been temporary promotions during World War II. They promised me that I would be assigned to my old unit[7] and that my first assignment would be at the Newark, New Jersey airport. Winnie and I seriously considered going back into the service. We did have trouble deciding because the rank of Staff Sergeant did not carry a very high pay rate in the 1940's[8]. We did know that they would pay our transportation and shipment of household goods if we were to be transferred. We made the decision to re-enlist in the Air Force.

I went to Newark Air Force Base on 3 May 1946 and re-enlisted in the Air Force for three years. I was paid a re-enlistment bonus; I was also paid a quarters and rations allowance and things were looking up.

At this point I went in to the Newark Western Union main office and told them that I was resigning. When they heard that I was going to quit they told me that they were very happy with my

---

[7] Airways and Air Communications Service

[8] The *monthly* salary plus allowances for a Staff Sergeant in 1949 (the oldest records available at the time of this writing) was only $199.70. That's less than $2400 *per year*.

work and that they would give me a raise. I told them "You are too late. I have already re-enlisted in the Air Force and there is no way that I can change my mind now. I am in the Air Force for a three year tour of duty." They told me that if I wanted to work part time with them while I was still in the Newark area they would be glad to accommodate me. I did manage to work for them on my off duty days while I was stationed at Newark. Financially we were immediately better off as a result of our decision to go back into the Air Force.

Soon thereafter, I received orders transferring us to Washington National Airport, Washington, D.C. departing on 19 June 1946. Upon our arrival in Washington, D.C., we searched for an apartment. We immediately learned that landlords would not rent apartments to people with children. We could not find an apartment in the Washington, D.C. area. We were able to locate a sleeping room in Alexandria, Virginia across the Potomac River from Washington, D.C.

My duty station was in the Air Force Communications Teletype major relay center at Washington National Airport. We lived in the sleeping room for a short time. We were then able to rent a mobile trailer home in Washington, D.C. After living only one month in the trailer it was sold and we had to move out. We rented a one-room cabin in the Washington Tourist Camp. There was no running water and no kitchen facilities in our one room cabin. Public showers and toilet facilities with running water were available near to our tourist cabin. Winnie cooked our meals on a hot plate, but we survived. The tourist camp was filled with servicemen whose families had children. We finally were all evicted from our cabins by the management. Winnie and Bonnie's picture was on the front page of the Washington Post newspaper with n article about our eviction. We were able to get into a newly established low rent apartment complex located on Blue Plains Drive in Washington, D.C. The complex was made up of numerous wooden reconverted World War II barracks. Our apartment was on the second floor. The apartment had a small kitchen equipped with kerosene stove and an icebox[9]. Occasionally, the pan overflowed

---

[9] The old type where you had to purchase a block of ice and place it in the top section.

and leaked into the downstairs apartment. We also had a living room where the fuel oil heater was located. We had one and a half bedrooms. The second bedroom was very tiny. We moved into the apartment during July of 1946. There was a row of fuel oil barrels in our front yard space, one for each apartment. We were very happy living in an apartment again.

My duty assignment during the period that I was assigned to Washington National Airport was as shift supervisor in the Air Corps Major Teletype Relay Station. Headquarters of the Airways and Air Communications Service (AACS) was located at Washington National Airport at that time. This was my first exposure to Teletype relay station operation. I worked shift work around the clock on a rotating basis. Occasionally I was called upon to operate the Teletype equipment in the AACS headquarters conference room to operate the communications equipment necessary to send and receive messages to conduct conferences between the AACS HQ and their various Wing Headquarters.

I worked as a shift supervisor in the tape relay station for months. I was to be upgraded to NCO in Charge of the Teletype Major Relay Station when the position became vacated due to personnel transfer of the previous NCO in Charge.

The Airways and Air Communications Organization was still new to the relay station business. During my assignment as NCOIC, I able to visit the Army Signal Corps Major Relay Station in the Pentagon located in Washington, D.C. on numerous occasions. I made a few friends there who allowed me to operate their equipment. I observed their methods and procedures enabling me to adopt and implement proven techniques in our own Air Corps Major Relay station at Washington National Airport.

Headquarters AACS moved from Washington National Airport to Andrews AFB, Maryland. Shortly thereafter, our Major Relay Station was also moved to Andrews AFB. We were on the first floor of the new Headquarters AACS Building. This actually enhanced our opportunity to get to know the Headquarters personnel and also for them to get to know us. My family and I did not have to move from our apartment at Blue Plains Drive. Although physically closer to Washington National Airport, the trip to Andrews was easier from that apartment; this made it an easy decision to stay where we were.

On 22 March 1948 Winnie went for a visit at Walter Reed Army Hospital in Washington, D.C. and was diagnosed as being pregnant. The doctor at Walter Reed gave her an expected delivery date of 10 October 1948. When Winnie woke up on 20 November 1948 she said "I am going to have the baby today." She was in no hurry to go to the hospital right away. She said, "I will let you know when I am ready to go to the hospital." She waited until after lunch to tell me she was ready to go to the hospital. We had made arrangements with our next-door neighbor, Stanley Vetula, to drive us to Walter Reed when she gave the word. We lost no time and departed for the hospital. When we arrived at the hospital we checked Winnie in and took a seat in the waiting room adjacent to the delivery room. They wheeled Winnie into the delivery room and after a period of time (I do not remember how long) they wheeled Winnie and the baby out. Winnie presented me with my son, and they were all cleaned up and in good shape. I was extremely happy that everything was okay. Frank Edward Parenteau was born on 20 November 1948. Bonnie was staying with her grandparents, Frank and Mabel McCairns in New Jersey for a while, waiting on the birth. I immediately went to the telephone and notified Bonnie that her brother was born and that Mom and the baby were both in good health. They brought Bonnie home shortly thereafter.

During my time at Andrews I was the NCOIC of the communications station providing service to the Pentagon, Newfoundland, the Azores, and the tributary stations connected to Andrews AFB. Our message center also served Headquarters AACS. Headquarters utilized me personally on their Exercise Emergency Communications support team in the underground alternate headquarters for Congress, the President and his staff in case of an unexpected attack. I was also used once to provide communications support to Strategic Air Command (SAC) Headquarters during one of their exercises. A Headquarters AACS Operations Captain and I made that trip together; it was an interesting trip. I was well liked by AACS HQ operations people and got along well with the Headquarters AACS Chief of Operations at the time, Colonel Lounsberry.

Another experience I had while NCOIC of the Relay Station at Andrews was the accidental motorcycle death of one of my shift supervisors. I was tasked with taking his body home to his parents who lived in Oklahoma. Of course, I knew him well and he was a close friend of mine. There were people in the service whose primary duty was accompanying bodies back to their parents throughout the USA. They were trained in their duties. I was not trained, nor was I really briefed in what I was to expect. I was told where I was to meet the body and provided tickets for the trip. I said goodbye to Winnie and went to the Union Station in Washington, D.C. at the appointed hour. I had already gone through his personal effects and packed them in his footlocker for shipment to his parents. We left Union Station and I was told that the body would be put on the mail car and we would change trains in St. Louis. I was advised that I had a berth in a certain sleeper car. I considered the possible ramifications, or should I say possibilities. What would I do if I got off the train in St. Louis and my friend's body was mistakenly off loaded somewhere between Washington D.C. and St. Louis? I told the conductor that I would stay the night in the mail car with the body. I sat up and watched the casket all night. When we off loaded the casket in St. Louis I accompanied it to where they placed it for the rest of the night. To my surprise there were about 50 other caskets in the same area. Now there is no way I am going to leave him here alone. I stayed the rest of the night in that area. I was the only living person with those fifty or so caskets in that area for the rest of that night. In the morning I accompanied Staff Sgt. Shuman's casket as they loaded it onto a train going to his hometown. Again, I rode in the baggage car until we arrived in his hometown in Bartlesville, Oklahoma. Fortunately, there was an undertaker to meet me at the station when I arrived. We rode to the funeral home along with the hearse. They took the casket inside and the undertaker, Sgt. Shuman's father, mother, and I stood and watched the casket being opened and I breathed a sigh of relief when I saw that I had made the trip and it really was Sgt. Shuman in the casket.

I took part in Sgt. Shuman's funeral. I presented the American Flag to his mother at the burial site. Sgt. Shuman's father was a minister. He was active in a local protestant church in Bartlesville, Oklahoma. He and Sgt. Shuman's mother were divorced. She had flown to Bartlesville and stayed with Sgt. Shuman's father in his home. Pastor Shuman had made arrangements for me to stay at the home of one of his parishioners while I was in Bartlesville.

When I went to the house where I was to stay I was surprised to find that one of the occupants of that house was a M/Sgt.[10] in the USAF and was in fact on leave at his home in Bartlesville. I also found out that he was in the same command as I, the AACS Communications Service. I had found out from a regular escort service man whom I met on the last leg of my trip to Bartlesville that the Air Force Person who accompanied a body home for burial normally stayed with the family for a period of two weeks following the funeral in case the family would need assistance. I stayed at the home of the M/Sgt. for two weeks.

One night the M/Sgt. and I were playing cards with members of his family in his dining room. All of a sudden we heard sirens near his house. We looked out to see the Oklahoma State Police with spotlights searching all over his property. We all lay down on the floor and waited; I had no idea what was happening. Finally, the doorbell rang and the M/Sgt. peaked out and saw that it was the police. They spoke for a few minutes and then the police left. At that point the Sgt. told me that he knew what was going on and that he would explain the situation to me.

He explained that his sister had married a man who had taken her to Mexico to live. When they got to Mexico that man had forced her into white slavery. She was kept under guard to ensure that she did not escape for an extended period of time. She later escaped and returned home to Bartlesville and was living in their home. I had seen her but was not familiar with her situation. At that point, he told me that the man might try to kidnap her again. He also told me that the Oklahoma Police had orders to kill him if he ever turned up in Oklahoma again. The police had a report that he may be in the area, so they came to find out. At that time the M/Sgt. pulled up his trouser leg and opened up his leg holster and pointed at his .45 caliber pistol in the holster. That was the end of

[10] Master Sergeant, one pay grade above Tech Sergeant.

our card game and I left the next morning for Andrews AFB on the first available train.

JAMES E. PARENTEAU
BORN 4 NOVEMBER 1921
SUPERIOR, WISCONSIN
PART 4

CHAPTER 9

BACK UP NORTH

I received special orders transferring me to the AACS Wing Headquarters located at Fort Pepperell Newfoundland sometime in September of 1948. I was unable to get a concurrent travel authorization to take Winnie and the two children, Bonnie Ann and Frank with me. Colonel Lounsberry told me that he had made arrangements with the Wing Commander in Newfoundland to have me transferred to Harmon Air Force Base for my tour of duty. I knew that the Air Force had quarters for enlisted personnel at Harmon AFB and that there were enlisted personnel who were allowed to have their dependents join them as soon as they found civilian housing near the base. We would then be able to apply for government housing on the base. How long we would have to wait until government housing was available would be another story. We would at least be able to be together again. Winnie made one thing clear; she said "I do not want to stay in a place that is not fit to live in. I had enough of that to last me a long time during World War II."

I traveled to Pepperell AFB by air transportation. I met the Wing Commander and was advised to take about a week off and learn my way around the organization there. I was surprised to find out that the Wing Commander was the same Colonel I had met in Nome Alaska in the 1940's. He was the Colonel who was instrumental in having me transferred from Nome, Alaska to Prince George during the 1940's.

A few days later I received word through the grapevine that I was going to come out on special orders transferring me to Lages, an island where we had communications facilities. I passed the information to Colonel Lounsberry and just waited to see what would happen. A week later I received a copy of my orders signed by the Wing Commander transferring me to Harmon AFB, Newfoundland. I traveled by Air Force transport again, this time to Harmon AFB, Newfoundland.

I was introduced to the commander of the 1931st Communications Squadron, Major Hughes, who advised me to report for duty to the Officer In Charge of the communications center, Captain Hodges.

I reported to Captain Hodges who explained to me that he had a T/Sgt. as station chief and really didn't have anything for me to do. He said I could come in and hang around the coffee room from 8 AM to 5 PM. This went on for some time.

I was living in the AACS barracks and eating in the mess hall. During the next few weeks, people in the barracks would come up to me and ask if I was working for the Office of Special Investigations. I would tell them that I was not, "I am just a T/Sgt. who was stationed at Andrews Air Force Base in charge of the Major Relay Station there." I could tell that they didn't believe me. I knew that all of my fellow military personnel had heard rumors about me, but I had no idea what they were saying about me.

I looked for housing in the town of Stephensville, Newfoundland. There was really next to no place for rent that looked fit for an American to live in. Some of our communications personnel were living in reconverted chicken houses. I advised Sgt. Jones at Andrews via our direct Teletype line to call Winnie and tell her what I have found as far as housing availability was concerned. She told Sgt. Jones to send me a wire. "Tell Jim to find the best housing he can find. I am ready to come to Newfoundland as soon as possible even if I have to live in a tent." I went to town looking for housing every chance I had.

There was one place that I knew of which might have possibilities. There was an old hotel about 5 miles from the base that had some apartments. Mr. Gallant was the owner. I looked him up and found out that Captain Hodges[11] was actually living in one

[11] The Officer in Charge of our Comm Center

of the apartments. I also found that there was a large beer hall that he was closing to convert into three more apartments. I looked them over and here is what I found:

The largest apartment available was in the reconverted beer hall. It had a tiny kitchen with running water piped into the sink. However, there was no pipe below the sink to carry the water out of the apartment. We would have to keep a bucket under the sink and carry the bucket to the one bathroom shared by two other apartments off the hallway to dispose of the water. At least it had running water and a pipe that led to the sewer. In our kitchen / living room we had a large room which would contain a couch and a kitchen table.

We used the sink to wash up and when we took a bath we used a washtub. One other problem was that the walls separating the apartments did not reach the high ceilings. The walls were about 12 feet high and then above that about a two foot space was open between the apartments. I believe the reason for the opening was to allow heat to circulate between the entire space of the old beer hall.

Mr. Gallant also owned the reconverted chicken houses. I saw one of them but would never have rented one of them for my family. I do not recall how much the rent was for the apartment. I signed the lease with Mr. Gallant and he explained to me that the Base would not allow him to charge as high as he required but that the military personnel renting from him gave him an extra amount under the table which he required before he would sign the lease. I agreed to accommodate his needs. The lease was signed and I had an apartment. I told Captain Hodges that I had rented an apartment in Gallant's Hotel. Captain Hodges told me that he liked his apartment, but that the Air Force was very slow in the shipping of household goods. He said he had been able to get some furniture from the base but it was things like double bunks for beds (etc.).

The following day I contacted T/Sgt. Jones again and asked him to tell Winnie that I had found an apartment. I also asked him to tell Winnie that I would put in for a furlough in order come home and get her and the children. Then, we would be able to drive to Nova Scotia where we could board a ferryboat and go to Newfoundland. The automobile would also go on the ferry with us.

When we got across the water we would travel by train and our car would arrive in Newfoundland. There we could pick up our car and drive to Stephensville and our new apartment.

The next day I received a message from Sgt. Jones saying that Colonel Lounsberry was making a trip to visit Harmon AFB in Goose Bay, Labrador and the region headquarters in Fort Pepperell Newfoundland. He also said Colonel Lounsberry asked if there was anything he could do for me. I sent a message to him and said, "Tell him that I would appreciate it if he would bring my furniture with him."

In the meantime I found out that my request for furlough was approved. I talked to Sgt. Jones the next day and he told me that Colonel Lounsberry was going to bring my furniture on his visit to Harmon AFB. Sgt. Jones had made arrangements with Winnie to bring a truck to the house and transport the furniture to the Colonel's airplane the next day.

The next day I received a call from my Commanding Officer, Colonel Hughes, who advised me that my friend Colonel Lounsberry had told him to have me meet the plane with a truck to pick up my furniture. He also told me he would handle the arrangements to have a truck available there. My commander also made it very clear that I had better be there on time at 3 PM to meet the plane or I would be in trouble.

I was there and standing next to Colonel Hughes and other key personnel whom he had arranged to meet the plane. When the plane taxied up to our welcoming committee we all stood at attention and saluted Colonel Lounsberry. The Colonel staggered out of the airplane and yelled at the top of is voice "Parenteau, come on up here and get your *%# &%!& furniture!" He obviously had been drinking heavily. I left the lineup and went right up and got on the plane. Colonel Lounsberry said, "I had a beautiful trip up here, I slept on your couch the whole way." He then left to join my commander. They departed and the detail of men drove the truck up to the plane and we transported my furniture out to my new apartment.

The next day when I went to work Captain Hodges, my officer in charge, let me know that he was not the least bity happy that I had received my household goods. He had been waiting a long time to receive his and still didn't know when they would arrive.

My next job was to go to the orderly room and pick up my leave papers so that I could fly home and later return with Winnie and the children. I was then told that I should report to the Commander. I knocked on his office door and he said, "Come in." I gave him a salute and told him that I was told to see him about my furlough. He said, "Your friend had other plans for you. He wants you to travel around to the various sites with him and he will fly you back to Andrews AFB with him." I said, "Colonel, I would much rather just fly back on my own directly home on furlough." The Colonel replied, "You do not have any choice in the matter. When Colonel Lounsberry leaves here you will leave with him." I thanked him and he excused me from his office.

I waited around for a few days and then was told that we were departing for Fort Pepperell, Newfoundland. We stayed a couple of days at Wing Headquarters. I stayed in the barracks with the enlisted Sergeants who traveled as crewmen with the plane.

One evening I was sitting on my bunk shooting the breeze with the crew. One of the men said he had been shacking up with a real nice girl in Congress Heights whose husband was a GI overseas. I asked, "What is her address?" He replied, "It is 750 something on Yuma Street." I jumped up and told him it had better be 750 something because my wife is living at 750 Yuma Street. He said, "I have the address in my wallet right here." He pulled out his wallet and the address was 752 Yuma Street. That house was across the main road and down the street, quite a distance from our house.

The following day we prepared to leave Ft. Pepperell for Andrews AFB. I had told Winnie that we could be flying to Westover AFB in Massachusetts to clear customs and then on to Andrews. I watched Colonel Lounsberry and other officers of the Wing Headquarters unloaded cases upon cases of Canadian liquor onto the plane. I found out that this was the holiday liquor run. Headquarters AACS gave the Colonel their orders and everyone involved would have a good supply of alcohol for Thanksgiving, Christmas and New Years Eve. They got the best liquor available in

Canada at a much more reasonable price, and their intent was apparently to skip around the US Customs Officer en-route.

When our plane was half way to Westover our pilot requested a change of flight plan to land in New York and go through customs and then take off for Andrews. I don't know what airport we were at, but assumed that we were waiting for the Customs Officer to come. The Customs Officer never arrived and after a long stop we took off for Andrews. I had told Winnie what our expected time of arrival was so she had gone to the Andrews flight line to meet us. After she had waited a long time she asked what time the flight would be arriving from Westover AFB. She was told that there was no flight from Westover scheduled to arrive at Andrews. She and the children waited, but finally had to give up and go home. When I got to Andrews I was able to call her and have her come get me. It was great to be home again for a visit.

We had a nice visit, but Frank didn't want to let me out of his sight. He thought I would leave and never come back, I guess. We packed our belongings and shipped the rest of the household goods through the normal channels to Newfoundland. We bought a new 1951 Plymouth and drove to New Jersey to spend Thanksgiving with Mabel and Frank McCairns. We said goodbye and resumed our trip to Nova Scotia where we would catch the ferryboat and take the overnight crossing to the mainland of Newfoundland. Our automobile was placed onto a flatcar and we rode the train to Stephensville Crossing. We then drove our automobile to Stephensville, Newfoundland and our new apartment home in the Gallant Hotel.

I had installed the double bunk beds in the very small room adjacent to the living room. I pushed them back against the sidewalls, which left an aisle of about twenty-four inches between the two beds. We stacked the boxes that we had carried up to Newfoundland in our automobile in the walking area located between the two stacks of beds. Bonnie and Frank slept in the lower beds and Winnie slept up over Frank's bed while I slept over Bonnie's bed. We set the alarm so that I could get to work on time, and went to bed. Early the next morning the alarm went off and I immediately stepped out of the top bunk to turn off the alarm. I crashed into the boxes that were stacked up below. I guarantee that was not a pleasant awakening.

We did not have an icebox or a refrigerator. We overcame that problem by getting an apple box and putting our food storage inside the apple box. We Jerry-rigged a wooden door so we could secure our stored food. We were told that the sheep that wandered around wherever they pleased would come up on the porch sometimes. Not long after that, one morning when I was leaving for work I found a sheep standing by our open apple box door eating the leg of lamb that Winnie had purchased at the base commissary. We then bought a lock and made sure that our apple box was secure.

We were happy in our new quarters and with the opportunity to be living together as a family again. We found a girl living across the road who would be happy to babysit our children so that we could go out to the NCO Club whenever we wanted to go out for the evening.

My problem with the commander, Major Hughes, continued to recur. He received a request from Headquarters AACS to send an individual to Andrews AFB for two weeks. I received a telephone call telling me to report to Major Hughes, which I did. He told me that sine I was their friend that I was selected to make the trip. He did not brief me on the purpose of the trip at all.

I packed my suitcase and picked up a copy of my travel orders and boarded an airplane and flew to Andrews AFB. When I arrived, I signed in at the Headquarters and went to the Operations section. Every person who I met was happy to see me again. At the end of the day I went to visit people I had known in Maryland and stayed there for the weekend. On Sunday morning Mrs. Wilson woke me up from a nap to tell me I had a long distance call. I thought it was Winnie calling me, but it was Bonnie on the phone. I talked with her for a while and then asked her to put Mom on the phone. She said that Mom and Frank had gone to church and that she wasn't feeling well. When I asked her how she got a hold of me she said, "I figured that you would visit the Wilson's. So, I found their number and called you collect." I told her "Hang up the phone and do not call anyone else before your mother returns from church."

I then hung up and called the operator, told her what had happened and asked her to contact the telephone operator back home. I asked her to call Winnie at a time that I knew she would have returned from church and tell her what had happened. I also asked her to have the operator back home to see that she doesn't make any more collect calls until her mother gets home. The operator took care of the situation and so did Winnie when she got home from church.

On Monday morning I went back to Headquarters AFCS Operations and was walking past Colonel Lounsberry's desk. He looked up and saw me and said, "What are you here for?" I replied, "I don't really know, I wasn't given any instructions. I was told to go to AFCS for two weeks and I came." When he told me he was going to call Colonel Hughes and see what was going on I asked him not to because I was in trouble with the Colonel all the time already. This was because Colonel Hughes never got over Colonel Lounsberry brining my furniture up to Harmon AFB for me. He said, "Okay, if that's how you want it, just stay around for the week and then fly back to Harmon AFB." I did as he said.

When I reported back to work after returning to Harmon AFB I was told that I was to go report to Colonel Hughes. I did so and Colonel Hughes told me that I was to go back to work and that I had better not give him any more problems or he would have me digging ditches for the rest of my tour in Newfoundland. I advised him that he could put me to work digging ditches or whatever he pleased and that I would do the best job he had ever seen. He excused me and told me to go back to the Communications Center for duty. I never knew if Col. Lounsberry called him or not.

Less than two weeks later I was told to report to Colonel Hughes again. When I reported to him he advised me that I was being sent to Iceland for three months temporary duty to help that relay station out. My orders would route me to the Wing Headquarters and on to Iceland. I said, "Colonel, I just brought my wife to Harmon recently and haven't had much time to really get her situated. I don't think this is fair treatment." The Colonel just said, "That is too bad. Here are your orders. You will leave Monday." I went home after work and gave Winnie the word. We decided that enough was enough. It was a hard decision, but we thought it was time to stand up for ourselves and get out of the service if necessary and look for a job somewhere else. I explained how I would accomplish the task at hand.

I followed orders and went to the Wing Headquarters and reported in. I then asked for permission to see the Wing Commander. I reported to the Wing Commander and he said, "Jim, we are going up to Iceland to get that Communications Station straightened out." I let him talk until he was finished. I then told him that it sounded good but that I had made up my mind to get out of the Service and that I would like him to call the Guard House and ask them to come out and put me under arrest because I was going to get out of the service one way or another." He said, "What is your problem?" I then told him the story from the day that Colonel Lounsberry told me he was coming to Newfoundland and asked me if there was anything he could do for me.

When I stopped talking the Wing Commander grabbed his telephone and said, "I will straighten him out." I said, "Please don't do that, I am in deep enough trouble with him and I have no desire to get into deeper trouble."

The Wing Commander put down the phone and said, "Jim, I want you to take a week off and visit here. When you take the train back to Harmon Air Force Base everything will be taken care of and you won't have any more trouble. You will not be going on temporary duty to Iceland." I thanked him and did as he suggested. Of course, I called Winnie on the telephone and told her what had happened.

I arrived back at Harmon AFB and went home to Gallants Hotel. I reported to duty the following day and Captain Hodges advised me that I was now NCO in charge of the Communications Facility located in the Base Commander's Headquarters building. I was now the NCO in charge of the Base Commander's Message Center. I never really had any problem again as a result of being a friend of Colonel Lounsberry or any trouble with Colonel Hughes at Harmon AFB. Later, when the other T/Sgt. was transferred I took over as NCO in charge of the Harmon Switching Center under the command of Captain Hodges. I had no knowledge of how things became straightened out, but I have no doubt that the Wing Commander handled the details. I remained assigned to the 1931 AACS Squadron.

CHAPTER 10

RHIP – RANK HAS ITS PRIVILEGES

Winnie and I went shopping in the Base Exchange[12] store one day and located a complete set for eight of Wedgewood China made in England. The price was out of our range. However, everyone was aware that if the merchandise in the base exchange stayed on the shelf too long the price would drop every week or so. We decided to keep our eyes open and if the price dropped we would love to have this set of dishes. We continued to check on the dishes for some time. One Saturday morning we went into the BX and low and behold the price had dropped into our range. We immediately found a clerk and asked her to pack the Wedgewood into boxes and we would take them home. She got busy and started packing the dishes into boxes for us to take home.

About ten or fifteen minutes later "Major Reno" the 1941 AACS Squadron Operations Officer[13] walked over to me and said, "Sgt. Parenteau, I have had my eye on that set of dishes for weeks. My wife came here today to purchase them. I want you to let us purchase them." I replied, "You are too late, Major. My wife and I have already purchased them and we are not going to change our minds about buying them." Major Reno was not happy with my response. He never approached the subject with me after that. However, he was the person to put his endorsement on my annual appraisal and my next one was the one and only unsatisfactory appraisal I would ever have in my entire 20 years of military service. His specific comments were "T/Sgt. Parenteau allows his personal family matters to take precedence over his military responsibilities." I got his message but didn't challenge his comments because I couldn't care less. We have enjoyed using the set of dishes and the complete set is in our China cabinet to this day.

Approximately six months into our assignment Winnie's mother and dad wrote us a letter saying that they were coming to

---

12 Also known as the BX

13 He was Captain Hodges' boss, who was in turn my boss

Stephensville to visit us. They were bringing their granddaughter, Cairn along with them. We knew that there was no way we could handle three visitors in our small apartment, but we really wanted to see them. We started looking around for better housing. We located a small house that we considered to be in a better location. The house had more space, but it had its drawbacks also. We had a pump adjacent to the kitchen sink so that if you pumped the handle you could say that we had running water. The sink had an outside drainpipe but we had no inside toilet facilities. Our company came and we made it through the visit. While they were visiting we took a trip by car to Cornerbrook, Newfoundland. It was a city many miles north of Stephensville. Cornerbrook was a much larger, more modern city than Stephensville.

We took the children fishing and picnicking often. There was one place where there was a scallop shellfish facility. Whoever ran the operation would obviously remove the scallop from the shellfish and discard the scallop shell onto the ground nearby. We would have fun picking out the prettiest shells that we then used for ashtrays. We also took picnics and went along the beaches and dug for clams. The clam would bury itself in the sand near the edge of the water and leave a small hole. We would dig wherever there were holes in order to find the clams. Winnie would not cook the clams that we dug, so we would carry them back to Stephensville where we would be able to give them to a Newfoundland family who loved clams.

One evening we hired a baby sitter to stay with Frank and Bonnie while we went out to spend the evening at the NCO Club. During the evening we were called to the telephone. It was our baby sitter telling us to come home immediately. We rushed home and found that Bonnie had been cut just below her left eye. We rushed her to the medical facility where they bandaged her up and we went home. Bonnie told us that she and another girl were inside the outhouse and a boy was harassing them and they were very afraid. He couldn't get inside and it got quiet, so Bonnie unlocked the door and peeked out to see if it was all clear. When he did, he slashed blindly at her and cut her face just below her left eye. Winnie wanted to call the Mounted Police, but I talked her out of it because I feared retaliation since we were in a foreign country. In retrospect, I believe that was one of the worst decisions I have ever made in my life.

CHAPTER 10

A TASTE OF THE COLD WAR

Soon we were assigned Base Quarters in a beautiful three bedroom house on Harmon Air Force Base. This was the first time I had been provided Base Housing since I went into the military service.

The housing was enlisted NCO housing. We had a nice kitchen and dining room and a large living room. There was also a nice basement. We were able to have a Ping-Pong table in the basement. The children went to school on the base. We were also able to obtain a local Newfoundland girl in her twenties who would live in and provide a permanent baby sitter for our children, washing, ironing and house cleaning for thirty dollars a month. Winnie did the cooking for us. I took a part time job as night manager for the base bowling alley and made some extra money for the family.

Living on the base was great. We were able to get fresh milk flown in and delivered to our quarters. The dining room had built in shelves with glass sliding doors to display our special China. We had a base operated telephone system and all the comforts one would expect in the USA.

One special Friday night at about 11 PM the sirens started blowing the emergency warning system. We were trained to have the airmen go to the AACS barracks to obtain their carbines and live ammunition and report to their duty stations for further assignment as required to protect the base facilities from the enemy. The women were trained to pack their necessary belongings for themselves and their children and be ready for pickup by the base busses and be taken to the flight line and airlifted back to the USA. Winnie and I were playing cards with the Cable family across the street. We tried to confirm that this was the real thing on the telephone, but the system was overloaded with everyone trying to do the same thing.

We kissed our wives goodbye, put on our fatigues and took off to get our rifles and ammunition. I was assigned to protect the entrance to the communications facilities. I challenged all personnel coming near the entrance to the Comm facilities, and I knew every person who came anywhere near the area that I was guarding.

The NCO club was always very crowded on Friday nights. We thought there would be a problem if they were drinking heavily and running around the base. It was a dark night. I could hear guns going off in the wooded area nearby. I was concerned about our people. Were they shooting at each other in the wooded area, or had enemy troops really landed? Did the women and children make it off the base? We stayed at support areas until the all clear was signaled at about 4 in the morning. Winnie had packed the suitcases with clothing for her and our children, but no busses came to pick them up.

The information that we received the following day was that the DEW Line[14] intercept facilities had alerted everyone that there was an aircraft headed for the USA coming into our area. After the initial warning everyone had lost contact with the DEW Line facilities. So, we implemented our special plans. I was sure glad to get the information that there were no casualties from friendly fire on our base. This was the only time our base implemented our Emergency Warning System.

Our tour of duty was scheduled to end in two years. I really wanted to go back to Andrews AFB for further assignment. Primarily, because we enjoyed the area and it usually would mean a longer stateside assignment. I was notified that my new assignment orders had arrived. I was to report to Headquarters AACS at Andrews AFB.

---

14 Distant Early Warning Line, a system of radar stations in Canada and Alaska designed to detect incoming Soviet bombers and provide early warning for a land-based invasion during the Cold War.

JAMES E. PARENTEAU
BORN 4 NOVEMBER 1921
SUPERIOR, WISCONSIN
PART 5

CHAPTER 11

CHIEF WARRANT OFFICER

I arrived at Andrews Air Force Base and reported for duty to Headquarters AFCS. I was briefed that I would work in the Traffic Analysis Section. I met the Officer in Charge of the section, Captain Radu, his secretary and Tom O'Brien, a Civil Service employee.

I worked in the Traffic Analysis Section. Shortly thereafter, I was assigned the responsibility of preparing an Air Force Manual to provide improved analysis reporting procedures by all USAF communications Centers to all applicable Command levels of operation. The Operations Section of AACS approved the manual. Subsequently, our Headquarters Operations Division established a conference in Hawaii inviting key operations personnel from the various Command Relay stations to attend. Our analysis personnel, Captain Radu and Tom O'Brien presented our manual and made a presentation explaining the new reporting procedures. The Air Force Manual was revised and an effective date of implementation was disseminated to all concerned. The procedures were implemented and used throughout the USAF Communications System. Hawaii was a beautiful place and we enjoyed the opportunity to visit.

My next big opportunity came when all Air Force Master Sergeants were notified that there were to be a large number of Warrant Officer's positions available in the USAF. We were notified that we would be advised when tests would be available to be taken by and M/Sgt. who wished to participate.

The first letter I received read:

Dear Sergeant:

Under the provisions of the Army, Air Force Authorization Act of 1949 and Armed Forced Reserve Act of 1949 and the Armed Forced Reserve Act of 1942, statutory authority was established authorizing the appointment of Warrant Officers as Reserves of the Air Force. Accordingly, the Air Force initiated a program designed to effect Reserve Appointments of Warrant Officers.

Budgetary and manpower limitations have resulted in the cancellation of that phase of the program which would have resulted in a call to extend active duty of the newly appointed Warrant Officers. In an effect to strengthen the Reserve Component, however, the Air Force is pursuing its original objective of effective Reserve Appointments of qualified individuals to the grade of Warrant Officer.

Then, a second letter read:

Dear Sergeant Parenteau:

I am pleased to report that your qualifications have been carefully evaluated and you have been selected for appointment as a Warrant Officer of the Air Force Reserve for an indefinite term. Enclosed is a letter of appointment, oath of office and a franked envelope. You may sign your acceptance of this appointment by completing the enclosed oath of office, and returning it to this headquarters with the least practical delay. The oath may be administered by a Notary Public or by an officer of any branch of the Armed Service whether or not he is serving on active duty.

The AACS Personnel M/Sgt. informed me one night at the NCO Club that I had made W-2 in the reserves. He also told me that if I dropped into his office the next day and initiated a request for active duty as a W-2 I could be able to come on active duty as Warrant Officer W-2 and would not be required to purchase my own uniforms. I did as he suggested and was recalled to Active

Duty as Warrant Officer W-2. My uniforms were issued to me and I was sworn in.

I was told that I would very soon have to go overseas but that I could pick my assignment. I talked it over with Winnie. I told her I would like to go overseas to the Philippines. She questioned me as to how long we would be separated if I were assigned to the Philippines. I informed her it would be 18 months. She asked how long we would be separated if I asked for Alaska. I had already spent time in Alaska, so I wasn't too anxious to go back there. We talked it over and we decided to request transfer to Anchorage, Alaska. Winnie then got the flu bug. When it became time to pack our household goods into boxes Winnie was still very ill and just laid on the couch and told me what to pack in which box. I packed everything including the dishes and the moving van picked up our furniture the next day. We left Washington, D.C. for Seattle in our automobile. I will not attempt to remember where we stopped overnight throughout our trip, but I will say that Winnie had a rough trip, stopping as necessary to get penicillin shots at medical facilities twice en-route. We drove across the Northern Route of the United States, picking up Route 2 West in Northern Michigan and continued across Wisconsin, Minnesota, North Dakota, Montana, and over the mountains into Seattle, Washington. We located the USS O'Hara[15], turned our automobile over to them and were provided a cabin on board while our automobile was carried on the ship as well.

We departed for Alaska via the Inside Passageway. We were required to participate in a lifeboat exercise shortly after lunch. I was then contacted by a Navy officer and advised that I had been assigned as the Ship's Duty Officer effective as of midnight that night. I was also told to meet two Navy officers in the dining room at midnight to accompany them on an inspection of the ship. I met them at midnight. On their inspection route we went below deck where approximately 50 to 100 soldiers were provided bunk beds in an open bay. The whole area was a complete unbelievable mess. The Navy officer in charge of the inspection ordered me to awaken these soldiers and see to it that this mess was cleaned up. The two

---

[15] A US Navy operated ship

Navy officers then departed the area. I awakened a large group and had them police the area and mop the floors, a big responsibility for a newly appointed Warrant Officer in the middle of the night.

We sailed to Seward, Alaska where the automobile and our family were transferred to a passenger train destined for the city of Anchorage. Our sponsor met us at the train and took us to a temporary apartment on the base where we stayed a short time before locating to a place to live in Anchorage. We lived at the Martin Arms Apartments for nearly a year before we were assigned to our Base Quarters on the hill in a beautiful house for the remainder of our tour of duty in Alaska.

CHAPTER 12

LIFE IN ALASKA

August 16, 1959

PARENTEAU'S NEWSLETTER

While the memories are still fresh I want to tell all of you about our wonderful vacation trip to beautiful Mt. McKinley.

At about 8 a.m. Wednesday morning on July 15th we left home for the Anchorage Depot to catch the Alaskan Railroad to Mt. McKinley National Park. We had two suitcases packed with all our clothes for the trip and a third suitcase packed with a heavy winter coat for each of us. We carried our camera gear. Winnie had the 8mm Movie Camera with 100 feet of film. Bonnie with her 127 Slide camera and film and Frankie with his 127 black and white film. I had the 35mm Slide camera with two rolls of film. We looked like Frank Buck and his "Safari" in "Bring 'Em Back Alive." Our ambition to "photograph the Alaskan Grizzly Bear." Keep in mind that the Bears have already killed four men in Alaska so far this season and you realize this is no easy project. We aren't really brave – but we believe that exercising due caution we should make out all right. We had a very nice train trip and arrived at Mt. McKinley at 4:30 p.m. that same night. The weather was pretty miserable. Frankie fed the Parka Squirrels in front of the Hotel and we took a few pictures (Slides and Movies). We confirmed our reservations for our guided tour through the Park (an eight our trip, one hundred thirty two miles). The tour was to start at 4 a.m. Thursday morning. We went to bed early and got up at 3 a.m. The next morning only to find that our reservations had been cancelled due to the fact that a bus broke down and the Hotel had over sold the trip. I raised heck with the manager and he assured me that I would be able to make the trip the next morning and return in time to catch the 12:30 p.m. Train back to Anchorage. He further gave his word that if we missed the train because of the change in plans we would be his guests for another day at no expense to us. I felt a little better about the mix-up since he made this promise but the trip was costing us a hundred dollars a day and I couldn't see paying that much and finding our reservations fouled up.

When the tour returned that day we found that they had only seen two moose. The weather had been very poor with rain and low clouds spoiling the view of the mountain. At this point I was happy we hadn't made that trip but we still had very little promise of the weather improving for the next day's trip in fact it may get worse. Winnie kept saying "Oh, don't worry tomorrow morning the sun will be shining real pretty."

The next morning at 2:45 a.m. I awakened and called Winnie. It was cold and raining outside. We awakened the children and at 3:30 a.m. We were eating Sourdough Hot Cakes and watching the rain outdoors. We hear that some of the guests were canceling their reservations due to the cold rainy weather. We bundled up in our warm coats and loaded on the bus. A short time later the rain stopped and soon a few patches of blue sky could be seen in the sky above. Our bus was full of people visiting Alaska from the South "48." About 25 miles out from the hotel we saw our first signs of wild life. At a distance so great that they could barely be seen with the naked eye were about thirty Mountain Sheep. They could be seen through the field glasses but it was useless to take any pictures. A little farther down the road someone in the front of the bus and Winnie about the same time shouted "Moose." We stopped and sure enough within about thirty yards there was a giant Bull Moose. He had a great big set of horns (we call it a rack). The people on the bus were really happy and we were mildly pleased because this was our first picture of a moose with a rack but we wanted Bear. We traveled along on our way and soon we got our wish – way off in the distance beyond camera range was a Grizzly Bear. A little farther down the road another couple of Grizzlies still out of range of the camera. Soon we saw one closer and took pictures but he was almost out of range of the camera and although we don't have the film back yet I am sure he was out of range of our camera. By this time the sun was coming out a little and the sky was clearing. All of a sudden three Caribou came into view along side our bus. We got out and took pictures of them. They were simply beautiful. I have never seen anything streak along as fast and yet as graceful as those three animals. We were glued to them with our telephoto lens and I promise you if our pictures reproduce what I saw through the viewer we will have some priceless pictures. I guess we took movies and slides of them. We were so excited I don't really remember. They were so close and well within camera range.

The peak of Mt. McKinley hadn't been visible for over a week due to low clouds and just about that time didn't one of the peaks appear majestically through the clouds, towering at a tremendous height of twenty thousand three hundred feet. I hung out the bus window and took a couple of pictures of the peak. I think I got so excited I took a couple shots of the road inside the bus before I got the camera out the window but you have to expect some losses. We pulled up to the halfway point of our trip and stopped for lunch after seeing Ptarmigan, Porcupine, Golden Eagles and much beautiful scenery. After lunch we drove back seeing more caribou, and bears at great distances. I finally dozed off and woke up to all the shouting of "Bear" "Bear" and in a heavy snow shower here within 25 yards of the bus was about a 600-pound Mother bear and two baby cubs. I got off the bus with about six or eight other people and took one slide shot and got back on the bus as I was getting back on the bus Winnie was getting off the bus with the Movie Camera – so you can see I wasn't off very long. Winnie and a man stood out there with the Bears and ground away with their Movie Cameras and Winnie says she took 25 feet of movie film of those three bears. Anyhow, she finished our 100 feet of movie film on them. Someone in the bus said "Boy, I'll bet those people would make a mad scramble onto the bus if that Bear started after them." The Park Managers had requested people stay on the bus if bear were seen. The guide said he had never seen Bear that close during his entire time in the park. Meantime old Mother Grizzly just looks around and eats a few roots in the ground. When Winnie got back on the bus she asked how many slides I got. When I told her she grabbed the slide camera and took some more slides out the bus window. So we got our Bear and during a July 17th Snow Storm at that. We haven't seen any of our film but hope it all turns out okay.

We returned to the Hotel at 12:00 p.m. And made the train back to Anchorage at 12:34. We had a real nice trip home on the train and were all pretty tired by the time we arrived back in Anchorage. One experience we had on the train before I close. Winnie, Bonnie, Frank and I decided to walk back to the Club Car for a coke and to listen to a few songs on the Juke Box. When we got back to the club car, here was an old Eskimo Squaw standing there. She had on a man's shirt and an old pair of blue jeans and was short and fat. A real dumpy, pretty sad looking female. She was high as a Georgia Pine, hind of a humming, mumbling, dancing the jig type of drunk. Winnie and the children sat down and I walked over to the Juke Box. I was looking over the selection of songs and the Eskimo gal hollered "Play number 27 for me." I looked at number 27 and it read, "Springtime In Alaska." So I dropped a dime in and played it. Boy that was my first mistake!!! I really made a hit with the doll. As the cowboys sang (?) her song, she sang portions of it to us. Between lines of which she slobbered over her beer. I waited my chance and told Winnie I was going to slip out, back to the coach. I was afraid she was going to follow me back to our coach. Well, by this time Winnie, Bonnie and Frank were in hysterics, laughing at me. So, I finally slipped out without her seeing me. If I had bought her a drink I would have made a friend for life. UGH!!!!!!!!

About a week after our trip our slides and movies came back. Our slides didn't turn out very well. Light got into the film somehow. When our movie film arrived there was a note inside which said, "Your film was damaged during processing as a result of an unusual accident. There was an error made in processing the film. We realize that the exposure of these rolls entailed considerable effort on your part and we are very sorry that these important pictures are spoiled." If they only knew!!!!! They refunded the price of new rolls of film. We cried for a few days at the loss of all our film but what can you do after the film is ruined. We should be grateful for the pleasure we did have during the exciting filming of our vacation to beautiful Mt. McKinley National Park and the Alaskan Grizzly Bear.

EPILOGUE

By James P. Parenteau

This is certainly not the end of the story; it is just where the written portion of the autobiography ends. Now I have the task of trying to finish telling my Poppa's story.

In May of 1959 the Parenteaus were transferred to Wright Patterson AFB in Fairborn, Ohio. They lived in a duplex for six months while they waited for their house to be built. They moved into their new home at 1840 Bordeaux Drive in November of 1959. Poppa retired from the Air Force in May of 1962. He started his new job at DESC two days later. He was the civilian manager of the first computer base ever to operate at an Air Force Base.

USAF Retirement

I was born in September of 1975. Just a short while later I developed laryngotracheobronchitis (croup). My parents were visiting Nanna and Poppa in Fairborn at the time and when I got so sick that I turned blue from a lack of oxygen they rushed me to Children's Medical Center in Dayton.

When we arrived at the hospital the staff were so helpful in dealing with my emergency that Poppa decided right then and there that he wanted to become a volunteer. Just as soon as he retired from the Civil Service he became a full-time (40 hours per week) volunteer at Children's Medical Center. One of his main jobs was to sit in the Children's Play Area, a waiting room full of toys where kids could play while they waited to see the doctor. He was so effective at this job that he influenced very many lives. On the next page is a copy of a greeting card he received from the mother of one of the patients he helped.

Poppa spent many years volunteering at Children's. I got the opportunity to spend a couple of summers volunteering with him at Children's. I had always enjoyed spending time with my Poppa, but it was during those summers that I got to know him a little better. He was truly a selfless giver of his time at the hospital. I am not surprised that he received many accolades as a "Voluntear," and should not have been surprised that he almost always refused to accept any of the awards bestowed upon him in person. That just seems to be the kind of person he was.

Playing with the kids at CMC

Dear Jim,

Here's a feather for your cap - what an accomplishment - my three-year-old Jesse wants to go to the doctor so he can "play with the man who eats checkers". He was so impressed by your tricks he's been telling everyone he knows about you. He's just about mastered flipping a coin from one hand to another.

We all enjoy your enthusiasm and wonderful way with children! Hope to see you soon!

Sincerely,
Connie, Ryan & Jesse Masin

Poppa's caring spirit was not contained to just the children at the hospital. He also cared deeply for his family, even though he seemed to have some difficulty showing it over the years. Here is a letter he wrote to Nanna for Christmas of 1993:

Merry Christmas Winnie 1993
When Did I Fall In Love With You?

My Darling Winnie:

When did I fall in love with you?
Was it on that warm summer evening in 1942 when I heard the automobile crash and helped you out of your car in the accident?

When did I fall in love with you?
Was it that first night I saw you in the ABC Club and invited you to have a drink with me at the bar?

When did I fall in love with you?
Was it the night I worked the midnight shift at the Connellsville Airport and sat and looked at your picture all night long? That was the night I decided to make you mine.

When did I fall in love with you?
Was it the warm summer evening I held you tight on your front porch swing and you told me for the first time that you were in love with me?

When did I fall in love with you?
Was it the night Tom Cline drove us to Oakland, Maryland where we found the preacher and were joined together in marriage?

When did I fall in love with you?
Was it when you arrived in St. Louis to visit me when I was away at Radio Mechanic School at Scott Field, Illinois?

When did I fall in love with you?
Was it on the train trip when you traveled as far as Cincinnati with me to say our goodbyes after I received my Overseas Orders to Destination Unknown in October of 1942, just three months after we were married? As I departed for the unknown and you returned home, we both considered the possibility that we may never see each other again.

When did I fall in love with you?
Was it on Christmas Eve in 1942 when we took a chance, defied Military Regulations, and you visited our Top Secret Base outside the USA? I sat in the house I rented and watched you walk up to our house because I couldn't chance meeting you at the railroad station. Was it as we stood in

the window the night you arrived and watched the beautiful snow scene together? I can see that snow scene any time I desire, because it is etched in my mind and always available when I feel the urge to reminisce. Was it when we hurriedly put you on the train to return home when the Lieutenant was apprehended for violating the same Military Regulations and rumors were out that he would be court martialled? When we had to say goodbye again after a beautiful two month visit.

When did I fall in love with you?
Was it when you arrived in May 1943 at Fort Saint John, British Columbia, after a 16 month separation, and presented our daughter, Bonnie Ann, age 8 months to me? You weren't even the least bit interested in playing cribbage that evening – were you?

When did I fall in love with you?
Was it when you presented our son Frank to me on November 20th, 1948 in Washington, D.C.?

When did I fall in love with you?
Was it when you stayed in the hospital with me for the entire month of September 1986 and nursed me through three heart attacks, heart by-pass surgery, and stomach surgery? You continued nursing me back to health during the ensuing winter months and years that followed.

When did I fall in love with you?
Was it when we sold our home and moved into the Bethany Lutheran Village to spend the rest of our lives together? A major decision which I couldn't have made without your support.

When did I fall in love with you?
Was it when we celebrated our 50th Wedding Anniversary at Bethany, on July 2, 1992, with our friends and relatives?

Knowing everything that I learned during our lifetime together, if I had it to do all over again, I would do it with you. One thing is certain, I will love you for eternity.

Merry Christmas,

I Love You,

Jim

Over the years Poppa's health began to fail. His mind deteriorated and he slowly left us. The last time I remember talking to him was in the summer of 2002. He was living in the Alzheimer's unit at Bethany Lutheran Village, where he would remain for the last few months of his life. I had had the opportunity to pursue my passion in aviation and was a First Officer with Comair Airlines based in Cincinnati, just a short drive from Dayton. My dad asked me to drive up to Bethany to visit with Poppa and wear my uniform. I was glad to oblige him and made the trip one afternoon after work. We didn't have much to talk about, I had already heard all of his stories a hundred times and even though I wished I could hear them all again he couldn't have told them to me even if he wanted to.

I tried my best to make small talk, but we just ended up sitting there enjoying each other's company as best as we could. Finally it was time for me to return home and as I was getting ready to leave he tugged at my sleeve and said, "This makes me happy." Little did I know those would be the last words my Poppa ever spoke to me.

Nanna's words describe it best when she wrote in her day planner on November 9, 2002: "Jim passed on to be with the Lord today." I had the privilege to share a few brief words at his funeral and here is a copy of my notes:

> Tom Brokaw called his the greatest generation. They were able to survive through the Great Depression; they banded together and defeated a powerful enemy in WWII… they came from all walks of life and put aside their feelings of individuality and led this country into a new era. That ***is*** an accurate definition of my grandfather's life.
>
> Just as importantly to me, is the experience ***I*** had with him in his later years. As the leaves are turning colors and making the scenery beautiful outside; so did his true colors show through in his autumn years.
>
> When I was a little baby I became very ill and my family had to rush me to the hospital. Poppa was so impressed with the volunteers at the hospital that he went in right

away and signed up. It was as if there was a war on and he was signing up for the military all over again. He spent many thousands of hours volunteering at Children's Medical Center; giving his time to children who were waiting to be seen by a doctor. I had the immense fortune to experience this with him when I was in high school and it was life changing. Did you ever see him with children? There was something about him; he had an effect on kids as he always tried to leave them with a smile. It was as though he was everybody's Poppa – always there to show you a trick with a "bug," or a broken checker chip, or a fake ketchup bottle. That is a bond that I know I will cherish for the rest of my life.

Mr. Brokaw also says that we should be sure to spend time with our members of the greatest generation. They are departing us at an increasing rate, and they are taking with them the stories of their lives. And if you ever had the time to sit with Poppa and hear some of his stories, you know how enjoyable that was. His stories were so good; I sometimes like to retell them myself. Like the one where he met this girl in a car accident when he was stationed in Connellsville, PA during WWII. And Nanna: I'm glad you guys met by accident. The Depression stories: working on a farm milking cows for free room & board. Or the mental picture I would always get when he told of how his father would throw a lump of coal off the train into the snow, and Poppa would have to go digging for it in its final resting place.

There are, of course, the stories you hear from other people about Poppa. Like how when he and his brother Jerry would go to a restaurant; between the two of them, their antics would ensure that the waitress would have a hard time.

So think on this today: Find someone who is over the age of 70, spend some time with them and ask them their stories.

There are many words I can think of to describe Poppa: He was self-effacing (I'm sure he would not enjoy hearing us speak so highly of him in his presence). He was interesting, engaging – always able to hold people's attention. He was compassionate – dedicating years of his life to adding a drop of sunshine into children's lives. But more importantly remember this: James Edward Parenteau was a man with character.

THE END

www.ingramcontent.com/pod-product-compliance
Ingram Content Group UK Ltd.
Pitfield, Milton Keynes, MK11 3LW, UK
UKHW041928190726
13854UKWH00004B/1507

9 780557 859788